Praise for *The Spiritual Dimension*

"For most of human history, leadership was inseparable from ˌ
power and cleverness. Paul Houston and Steve Sokolow's practical and down-to-earth
will help many find their way back."

—Peter Senge, Founding Chair, Society for
Organizational Learning, and Senior Lecturer, MIT

*"I can't imagine a more timely and important book for educators. Where do we find the courage
to continue? Where do we find peace when surrounded by aggression and corruption? What
sustains us so that we can remain strong in serving the interests of children? The answers to
these questions are in this book. The authors, with great wisdom and generosity of spirit, offer
the perspectives and practices that enliven and vitalize our spirits. They have given us more
than a lifeline—they have given us solid ground to stand on in the midst of turbulence."*

—Margaret J. Wheatley, Author
Leadership and the New Science

*"Being both a nonbeliever and a person wary of books whose titles suggest that there are eight
principles of leadership, I approached this volume with some trepidation. What I found was a
description of leadership that actually transcends the outdated idea that it can be reduced to a few
principles or that it can be acquired by learning some skills. Instead the book honors its complexity, casts it mainly in terms of creating sound relationships, and offers what I would call a posture
toward leadership, which I regard as far more valuable."*

—Richard Farson, President, Western Behavioral Sciences Institute, and Author
Management of the Absurd and *Whoever Makes the Most Mistakes Wins*

*"Houston and Sokolow have done an extraordinary job of looking beyond the traditional view
of leadership to incorporate a spiritual dimension. They show how enlightened visionary
leaders can use their own innermost spiritual principles to bring about the best in themselves
to create a working environment that builds on collaboration and sharing. It breaks down the
communication barriers that separated us—and builds on the essential concept of connectedness between and among people."*

—Gerald T. Tirozzi, Executive Director
National Association of Secondary School Principals

*"In order for teachers to empower their students, teachers must first be empowered themselves.
At a time when teachers are feeling frustrated and disenchanted, this inspiring and insightful
book offers a series of spiritual principles of leadership that can help empower both teachers
and students alike."*

—Reg Weaver, President
National Education Association

*"When I served as Governor of South Carolina, improving education was my top priority. As
U.S. Secretary of Education, I was honored to lead President Clinton's crusade for excellence
in education. Wise leadership, especially in education, is one of the keys to America's future
success. In this book, Paul Houston and Steve Sokolow sow seeds of wisdom that offer hope and
sound guiding principles for America's education leaders."*

—Richard W. Riley, Former U.S. Secretary of
Education and Former Governor of South Carolina

(Continued)

More Praise for
The Spiritual Dimension of Leadership . . .

"The Spiritual Dimension of Leadership *reminds us that the job of leadership is complex . . . but the actions we take can be very simple and yet have a big impact. There are valuable insights here for leaders at every level.*"

—Anne L. Bryant, Executive Director
The National School Boards Association

"*Finally, a book that examines leadership from a human perspective! Houston and Sokolow cut through all the leadership jargon and focus on how leaders can remain true to their core beliefs and still lead successful organizations. This should be required reading for all leaders and prospective leaders.*"

—Vincent L. Ferrandino, Executive Director
National Association of Elementary School Principals

"The Spiritual Dimension of Leadership *asserts that, like the creation of music, successful execution is not a matter of technique but a matter of inspiration and dedication to task, emanating from a courageous search for the core of one's being.*"

—Peter Yarrow, *Peter, Paul & Mary*

"*This book is loaded with insight into a crucial dimension of leadership.*"

—Scott Thompson, Assistant Director, Panasonic Foundation, and Author
Leading From the Eye of the Storm

"*In our attempts to improve education, we are snuffing out the very thing that would make it better—human spirit. This book fills a troubling void in the leadership literature by highlighting the vital spiritual side of a leader's role. Schools don't need any more testing; they need a big dose of zest, buoyancy, and meaning. Reviving the spirit is the critical challenge. This book shows us how.*"

—Terrence E. Deal, Author
Leading With Soul and *Reframing the Path to School Leadership*

"*I felt as though I was having a conversation with God when I read your book . . . as though I'd been blessed with the opportunity to touch the essence, the wonder, the silence of God's presence . . . it felt like a tear. . . . Is there a greater or more pure joy?*"

—Frances Hill, Associate Professor
Northern Arizona University

"*I know this book of wisdom will make a difference to the important people who care for our children in schools. . . .*"

—Kathleen Alfiero
Co-founder, i'monair

"*This book is* great! *The authors have taken a very slippery topic (spirituality and leadership) and made the connection from the spiritual roots to the practical fruits. It's seamless!*"

—Chuck Bonner, Assistant Principal
Great Valley High School, Malvern, Pennsylvania

PAUL D. HOUSTON
STEPHEN L. SOKOLOW

The
SPIRITUAL
DIMENSION
OF
LEADERSHIP

8 KEY PRINCIPLES TO LEADING MORE EFFECTIVELY

FOREWORD BY DAWNA MARKOVA

CORWIN PRESS
A SAGE Publications Company
Thousand Oaks, California

For information:

Corwin Press
A Sage Publications Company
2455 Teller Road
Thousand Oaks, California 91320
www.corwinpress.com

Sage Publications Ltd.
1 Oliver's Yard
55 City Road
London EC1Y 1SP
United Kingdom

Sage Publications India Pvt. Ltd.
B-42, Panchsheel Enclave
Post Box 4109
New Delhi 110 017 India

Printed in the United States of America

Library of Congress Cataloging-in-Publication Data

Houston, Paul D.
The spiritual dimension of leadership: 8 key principles to leading more effectively /
Paul D. Houston, Stephen L. Sokolow.
     p. cm.
Includes bibliographical references.
ISBN 1-4129-2577-0 (cloth)—ISBN 1-4129-2578-9 (pbk.)
   1. Leadership—Religious aspects. 2. Teaching—Religious aspects.
3. Religion in public schools. I. Sokolow, Stephen L. II. Title.
BL325.L4H68 2006
371.2′011—dc22   2005031685

This book is printed on acid-free paper.

06   07   08   09   10   10   9   8   7   6   5   4   3   2   1

Acquisitions Editor:	Elizabeth Brenkus
Editorial Assistant:	Desirée Enayati
Production Editor:	Melanie Birdsall
Typesetter:	C&M Digitals (P) Ltd.
Copyeditor:	Jacqueline A. Tasch
Proofreader:	Mary Meagher
Cover Designer:	Michael Dubowe
Graphic Designer:	Scott Van Atta

This book is dedicated to:

Steve's parents,
Cy and Charlotte Sokolow,

Paul's parents,
Paul Doran and Irene Houston,

and above all
to God

for our inspiration, calling, and gifts.

Contents

Foreword

Thank God our time is now when wrong comes up to meet us everywhere,
never to leave us till we take the longest stride a soul folk ever took.
                                                        —Christopher Fry

You are now holding a book that is remarkable for at least three reasons.
One is the men who wrote it, two is the way they wrote it, and three is
because of the time in which it is written.

Stephen and Paul are what poet John O'Donohue would call *anam cara*,
soul friends. They have known each other for over twenty years, but rarely
do they engage in small talk. There is between them a palpable energy that is
stronger than either one of them alone. The closest I can come to describing it
is what Martin Luther King Jr. would call "soul force." If you were to eavesdrop
on them in the front seat of a car, you would most likely be drawn into what
I call a "conversation of discovery." One of them asks the other a beautiful,
open question, the kind that cannot be answered and causes you to think
deeply. Instead of asking each other about the stock market or how much
money they are making, one of them more likely would ask, "Have you ever
thought about what is your real wealth?" This is followed by a long and hungry
silence. Each listens to himself as well as to the space between them. You find
yourself breathing a bit deeper, your chest opening, your periphery expanding,
as you wonder with them.

At exactly the right moment, one of them responds with a story from his
life. It doesn't answer the question at all but rather embraces it, exploring the
way you would find your way through the Maze at Chartres. That story evokes
another one in the listener, then one in you, then another question unfurls
until you have the delicious feeling of inclusion I can only call resonance. It is

---
Dawna Markova, PhD, is the author of *The SMART Parenting Revolution: Unleashing
Your Child's Potential* and *I Will Not Die An Unlived Life: Living With Purpose and Passion,*
co-editor of *Random Acts of Kindness,* and co-founder of Smartwired.org.

as if you have stepped onto a raft being drawn by a powerful current down a river which flows between two lush banks.

Stephen and Paul met while they were attending a professional seminar at Harvard University. They were both superintendents of school at the time. While you might assume that educational leaders would be ardent learners, in my experience, the opposite is often true. Most of us who teach have forgotten how to learn, and seminars at Harvard are more often places where people show off their mastery rather than environments for exploring the mystery of life. When Paul and Stephen met, two very different men from very different backgrounds, they sat on those opposite banks and found the passion of their lives joining in a river of spirit flowing between them, drawing them forward.

To truly appreciate them as well as this book, you have to be willing to dig down beneath the surface of things. Let's explore, therefore, the roots of the words we're using to describe them and their work. The origin of the word *professional* is *profiteri*, which means an avowal of faith or belief. The root of the word *educate* is *educare*, which means to draw out that which is within. The root of the word *to lead* is *laithjan*, which means to cause to go on one's journey. The word *spiritual* was derived from *spirare*, to breathe. The word *principle* was derived from *principe*, which means foundation. These two soul folk are involved—and want to involve you—in professing your faith in those who share the journey with you, finding the foundations that will enable you to draw out the best of that which is within by inspiring, aspiring, and conspiring together.

The third remarkable thing about this book is that it's written now, in a time of rigidity and fragmentation when we're all victims of the blame game, which puts us on opposite sides and polarizes us through either/or thinking. Along come these two very different men who ask each other questions that lead us toward solutions large enough to hold all perspectives; questions that can help us individually and collectively live, as author Parker Palmer would say, divided no more.

Most educators today feel suffocated under the rigidity of the standardized testing requirements that measure today's children by yesterday's standards for tomorrow's world. We are dividing the world into two opposing camps— the parents versus the teachers, the superintendents versus the school board members, those that have versus those that don't, the successes versus the failures.

Between these polarities is an abyss that grows deeper and wider day by day. Our children's future is perishing in that abyss. In the rampant fear that is being fostered in all of this uncertainty, we cling to the belief that a leader is someone who is certain. In these terrorized times, we have forgotten how to think for ourselves, how to design our way out of trouble—a phenomenon that arises from honoring each person's unique difference and capacity to imagine new possibilities.

The conversations Stephen and Paul have been engaged in for the last two decades—the open questions and musings and principles that are the foundation of this book—have created a bridge across the abyss. Out of mutual respect for their differences, as well as an honoring of the spirit of their shared values, they have transformed the noun *leadership* into the verb *leading*, drawing out the best that is within each one of us.

Both of the authors of this book have been leaders at the top of their field of education. In a storm, the top of a tree is the most dangerous place to hang out. You will be buffered and besieged, which is exactly what many of today's educational leaders are experiencing. In such a storm, it is necessary to crawl down to safety, down to the trunk of the tree, where you have something strong you can hold onto. Paul and Stephen do that by guiding us down to the principles and values that we can hang onto in the strongest winds until we find the stability we need to risk crossing to explore the other bank.

When I first saw the manuscript of this book, I thought, "Oh great, another fluffy-wuffy California spiritual treatise. How can this be relevant to me, as I work with children who come to school with rat bites on their faces and with parents who are deployed in Iraq and with teachers who have to falsify test scores so funding won't be taken away from their students? I am too busy to be bothered reading such a thing."

I had met Paul and Stephen a year before when they asked me to give a keynote speech at the yearly conference of AASA. I was reluctant. School administrators can be the most difficult audience to speak to—the image of thousands of arms tightly crossed over thousands of chests chokes me into silence. I went to dinner with them. I listened to these two friends talk, not about football scores or their golf game but about what could be possible for children if we all came together on their behalf. I left the restaurant feeling as if the ice that had made my own thinking rigid for decades was melting in the warmth of the "yes tunnel" that existed between them.

In case you don't know, a "yes tunnel" is a transformative moment of meeting. It is one where the connection between two people is present focused, noncritical, and fertile. Think of when you crouch in front of a 10-month-old baby and put out your arms, encouraging her to walk forward. Think of when you fell in love for the first time and, as Parker Palmer would say, "listened the other into speech." Neuroscientists are asserting that we are, in fact, hardwired to connect in this way, and when we do, the brain can make new synaptic connections and possibly differentiate stem cells into new neurons. In other words, creating "yes tunnels" between each other can help all of us to grow new possibilities that are larger than our problems and wide enough to bridge the abyss that lies between "either/or."

Enfolded in one of Paul and Stephen's "yes tunnels," I agreed to give that keynote address. They sat in the front row, eagerly leaning forward, pulled by their passion to learn, listening me into speech. It was that which drew me to actually read the manuscript of this book with an open mind. Ironically, I have recently moved to California because I could no longer breathe at Utah's altitude without an oxygen leash. Now I live in this fluffy-wuffy land of vineyards and oceans, and I breathe fully and freely. Breath has become all-important to me. Breath, *spirare,* spirit.

I am deeply moved and surprised by what I have read in these pages. It is not fluffy or wuffy. It is grounded in the practical wisdom of two men who have lived and are learning how to bring out the best in themselves and in others. It inspires me. It helps me let go of the limiting thoughts and beliefs in my mind that should have expired long ago. It includes me in a conspiracy that shifts the conversation from "What is the matter with our children, our school system, our teachers, our organizations, and our country?" to "What really matters about our children, our school systems, our teachers, our organizations, and our country?"

It is my delight and honor to introduce you to these two men, to this book, and to this remarkable "yes tunnel." May it help all of us create a bridge to a possible future for our children.

—Dawna Markova

Preface

Superintendents and other educational leaders rarely talk about what motivates them to do the difficult work that they do. Day in and day out, you fight to create the schools that your children need and deserve, but rarely do you talk about the values, beliefs, and principles that guide and inform your work and that sustain you in difficult times. When people say they are glad they don't have your job, they mean it. So, why do you do the work you do? The reasons, of course, are complex.

At a fundamental level, your work is an expression of who you are at the core of your being. You care about other people, especially children. You believe in education and its value to our society and to the children you serve. You thrive on helping others and on unleashing the potential in your staff so that they, in turn, can unleash the potential in children. Many of the values, beliefs, and principles that guide and sustain you have underlying spiritual roots. The more in touch you are with those spiritual roots, the more enlightened your leadership becomes and the more effective you are in leading others to a better future.

Given the complexities of the issues educational leaders face, it sometimes seems as though you need the wisdom of Solomon to determine the right course of action. The best way to think about the spiritual dimension of leadership is that it is based on wisdom. Where does this wisdom come from? It comes from within you. It is the divine spark that guides you as you live your own life and lead others toward a brighter future. Enlightened leadership is grounded in spiritual principles, and because of this, it brings out the best in you and in others. Not only do enlightened leaders know the right things to do—and how to do things right and at the right time—but also they do them for the right reasons.

There is much to be said for the difference between making a living and making a meaningful life. Far too often in our culture of consumption and being consumed with material things, people lose sight of those things that are truly important—friends, family, feelings, and faith. You may often find that you are so busy in your day-to-day life that you forget to live in accord with your inner guidance system.

Likewise, for leaders, the temptation is to be so caught up in the day-to-day challenges of the organization that you forget that organizations are made up of people and that to lead people, you must stay connected to that which is basic and constant. Both of us have spent our careers leading a series of complex organizations. We have been on the firing line of leadership virtually our entire adult lives. When you lead an organization, you dwell in the rarefied air of the mountaintop. It becomes easy to forget how your actions may impact others. You are also faced with the dilemma of taking care of the organization while knowing that you are constantly taking actions that may hurt some of the people in it. There is also the challenge of having to react to events as they fly at you, without having the luxury to take the time to step back and think about what you should do or why one path may be better than another and what values you might be ignoring in the process.

We started out as professional colleagues, school superintendents in school districts not far from each other. We came to know each other well as we attended a series of summer programs at Harvard University aimed at superintendents. As we talked about our challenges, our frustrations, and our victories, we found that most of the time, we weren't talking about education or even leadership per se—we were talking about our spiritual values and the underlying connections between who we were at the deepest level and what we did on a day-to-day basis. These discussions started us on a joint expedition of the soul that has led to a 20-year conversation on what it truly means to be a human being and the implications of that awareness for our work.

We came to identify 42 principles that we felt guided us and our work, and we have no doubt that there are many more. This is an open ended, evolving body of work. We selected eight of these principles to focus on in this book, not only because they are a good place to start and resonate particularly with school leadership, but also because they represent various aspects of the energy of mind, body, and spirit, or what we think of as the energy of head, hand, and heart. To us, these principles are spiritual not only because they are life enhancing but also because they focus on the interconnectedness and interrelatedness of life at all levels. As with anything in the spiritual realm, our respective understandings of these principles are works in progress—as are all human beings. These principles are not something you can check off on your "to do" list. They are habits of mind and soul that can act as guideposts for the perilous and wonderful journey we call leading. They must be approached with an understanding that you are never quite there and that you will often fall short in your efforts to apply them. But try we must.

A chapter in this book is devoted to each of the eight principles. The chapters begin with a brief overview that highlights the key elements of the principle. To develop the content for each chapter, we engaged in an extensive dialogue to uncover our shared wisdom and truth, based on our collective life experiences and those of people we know, both professionally and personally; on our shared reading lists, including most of the books listed in our selected bibliography; and on our individual and collective intuition, insight, and inspiration. We have divided each chapter into a series of subsections to explore the depth and breadth of each principle. Although we have spent the major portion of our professional lives as superintendents in the field of education, we believe that this book will be useful and helpful to prospective and practicing leaders in all fields, including the private sector, nonprofit organizations, and government. In each chapter, there are short stories to help illustrate aspects of that particular principle. For the most part, these stories are drawn from our professional and personal lives; they are all true, but in some instances, names or gender have been changed to shield the identities of the people involved. With practitioners in mind, we have included specific "Suggestions for Action" and a brief "Summary" at the end of each chapter.

We have sometimes been asked, "How do you apply these principles in your day-to-day work?" One example comes to mind. Most leaders and managers have been taught that delegation is an important managerial tool. Leaders can't do everything. They must enlist others in the work. This is managed through delegation. Few leaders, however, pause long enough to realize that if you can't trust the person to whom you have given the task, believing that they will carry it out and forgiving them for not doing it the way you would have, a thousand seminars on delegation will not allow you to fulfill the leadership function. So to be truly effective, you must dive below the surface to find the spiritual principles that allow you to bond with others, to find the connection between your work and your deepest self, and to be guided by wisdom that has been given to us by spiritual leaders since time began.

As we have discussed our work with others, we have found that people have a deep hunger to understand more about it. Quite evidently, most people have come to understand that the talk and action of our secular world must be anchored in something deeper and more profound. At some level, everyone knows that success can't be measured by the bottom line or by a test alone—it is written in your heart. So, even in the hard-headed world of management and leadership, there must be a sense that the "head bone" is connected to the "heart bone." There must be a ballast that allows your ship to sail upright. This book is an exploration of some of the principles that can create that ballast for leaders and help you understand that you can enhance your life and the lives of others in the midst of making a living.

Because the principles that we have illuminated in this book are straightforward and easy to understand, it is easy to underestimate their importance, power, and depth. In the same way that things are easier said than done, these principles are easier read than done. These principles are like spiritual muscles and, like your physical muscles, they must be used regularly and exercised to strengthen them and make them more agile. The more you embrace these principles and practice them, the greater the payoff will be, not only for yourself and for those you lead but ultimately for the world.

As you manifest the spiritual principles of leadership presented in this book: Intention, Attention, Unique Gifts and Talents, Gratitude, Unique Life Lessons, A Holistic Perspective, Openness, and Trust, you will find that you are becoming a more enlightened and effective leader—a leader who does the right things, in the right way at the right time, for the right reasons. Enlightened leadership is not an end in itself. It is a means of bringing more wisdom to you and to the organization you lead. And it is a means of shaping a better future for yourself, your children, and the world at large.

We have formed a center that will serve as an information network, a support network, and a forum for collaboration and training for people who are striving to become more enlightened leaders by increasing their attention to the spiritual dimension of leadership. If you are interested in learning more about the center and *The Spiritual Dimension of Leadership*, please contact us at: The Center for Empowered Leadership (www.cfel.org).

May we enlighten our own and each other's paths.

Acknowledgments

Bringing this work to publication has been quite a journey. It is a journey that Paul and I began more than 20 years ago when we started swapping books with spiritual and mystical themes at Harvard University's summer seminar for superintendents. The inspiration for the book was Paul's. In an unplanned, inspired moment during the summer of 2000, Paul asked me if I would like to co-author a book with him about the integration of spirituality and leadership. My heart said yes before my head realized what I was getting into. During the next few years, we co-wrote a seven-book series on the spiritual principles of leadership in a dialogue format, which was more than several publishers wanted to commit to printing. Lizzie Brenkus, acquisitions editor at Corwin Press, suggested we expand an article I wrote about the principles of enlightened leadership for the September 2002 edition of *The School Administrator* into a book sprinkled with applications and examples of those key principles. And here it is!

First I want to express my heartfelt thanks to Paul for an invitation that changed the course of my life. We have become dear friends and partners in a venture that reaches beyond the horizon. Thank you, Paul, for truly blessing my life in countless ways. We both want to thank Lizzie Brenkus and Robb Clouse at Corwin Press for seeing our work's potential to make a significant contribution to the field of educational leadership. And we both want to express our deepest gratitude to Dr. Dawna Markova, an internationally known author and educator at large who made our hearts sing with joy when we read her foreword to our book. It has perfect pitch. No one but Dawna could have written it. We are honored and humbled by her words. We love Dawna and look forward to partnering with her in building a bridge to our children's future. My well of gratitude runs deep with all of the people who have contributed to my life's path.

More than 30 years ago, Professor Lee Olson first introduced me to the spiritual underpinnings of leadership. He was and is a role model of what it means to live your spiritual values. I am indebted to him for his love and guidance and for being a living example of an enlightened leader.

My brother Adam is a psychotherapist, a mystic, and an advanced student of esoteric Buddhist teachings and philosophy. He is the wisest person I know. For many years, we have been taking weekly "walk 'n' talks" in Nature. He has been my guide, teacher, and executive coach. His wise counsel has been invaluable to my growth as a human being, and his spiritual insights have helped shape my own.

I am a Reiki Master and have been practicing Reiki for almost 15 years. Reiki is a form of divine energy that promotes healing and spiritual growth. I am indebted to Djuna Wojton, a wonderful human being and Reiki Master, who has shared her gift with me and countless others.

Alan S. Fellheimer, an attorney and a banker, is my closest friend, and this has been true our entire lives. He'll be embarrassed by this, but truth be told, he is the smartest person I know. More than 30 years ago when I was writing my first book—my doctoral dissertation—Alan taught me the craft of writing. Without his countless hours of tutorials, neither that book nor this one would have seen the light of day.

Dr. Muska Mosston is a deceased friend whose spirit I still carry in my heart. A distinguished educator and author, he was like a second brother to me during the 15 years when our lives converged. He loved the world of ideas, and he loved to write. As we talked about education and leadership, he continually urged me to write a book. He was the third in my rule of 3s to suggest that I attend Harvard's summer seminar for superintendents. Without Muska, I would not have gotten to know Paul Houston well, and someone else would be writing this acknowledgment.

Dr. Bea Mah Holland, along with Paul and me, is one of the founding partners of the Center for Empowered Leadership. She and Paul both received their doctorates from Harvard, and Bea has had a distinguished career in both the private sector and in the field of education. A former editor of the *Harvard Education Review*, president of a publishing company, and editor of *Appreciative Leaders*, a book about appreciative inquiry, Bea graciously edited this entire manuscript as a labor of love and friendship. Paul and I are truly grateful to her.

Saving the best for last, I want to thank my wife, Laney; our children, Brett and Brian; our daughter-in-love, Cori (Brett's wife); and our granddaughter, Gabrielle. For the past 15 years, Laney has taught gifted children at the elementary level as part of a teaching career spanning almost 30 years. While our children were young, Laney worked as a newspaper copy editor. She has always proofread my work, and proofing this manuscript was her latest labor of love. Laney, Paul and I appreciate you as a detail person with an eagle eye, and we thank you for putting our work in perfect shape. My children have been a continual source of growth for me and are the source of many insights incorporated into our work. Our work envisions enlightened leaders creating a better future for all of our children, and my granddaughter, Gabrielle, inspires me as one of those children. My family has given me the gift of their love and support, and I want them to know that I do not take them or their love for granted.

With heartfelt gratitude,
—Stephen L. Sokolow

We are all the sum of what has touched us, and anything I might do is the result of what others have done for me: There are far too many to mention. I would like to thank my father, who grounded my spiritual beliefs with a sense of grace and generosity. He was the best Christian I have ever known because he got the "word" and made it "flesh." My mother gave me my warrior spirit and the common sense necessary to navigate this temporal plane. The late Richard Green made me see myself as more than my past, and my "Tucson Gang" (Rog, Vee, Jack, Sue, Ross, Suzy, and Jesse) has been my family through thick and thin.

A number of spiritual guides have come to me when I needed them—the teachers who were there when the student was ready—and to each and all, I am most grateful. My children, Lisa, Suzanne, and Caroline, taught me that while we are connected to the Divine, that connection is played out in the chain of life that we receive and pass on to others; also, they make me laugh. I thank the Universe for my fiancé, Sandy, who proved that it all comes in the right time and space and who has encouraged this work and me to become all that God intended. Sherri is a key member of the village that continues to raise me. And finally, for Steve, whose focus and determination have kept this work alive and who has taught me more about spirituality and leadership than he might ever imagine.

—Paul D. Houston

Corwin Press gratefully acknowledges the following individuals:

David W. Magill
Director
Laboratory Schools
University of Chicago
Chicago, IL

Chuck Bonner
Assistant Principal
Great Valley High School
Malvern, PA

Edgar Gill
Associate Professor
School of Education and
    Behavioral Studies
Azusa Pacific University
Azusa, CA

Albert Armer
Principal
Wortham Elementary School
Wortham, TX

Joseph M. Giancola
Corwin Author
Kent State University
Kent, OH

Christa Metzger
Corwin Author
California State University,
    Northridge
Northridge, CA

About the Authors

 **Paul D. Houston,** executive director of the American Association of School Administrators since 1994, has established himself as one of the leading spokespersons for American education through his extensive speaking engagements and published articles, as well as his regular appearances on national radio and television.

After working at schools in North Carolina, New Jersey, and Alabama, Paul served as superintendent of schools in Princeton, New Jersey; Tucson, Arizona; and Riverside, California.

Paul has also served in an adjunct capacity for the University of North Carolina, Harvard University, Brigham Young University, and Princeton University. He is a consultant and speaker throughout the United States and overseas, and he has published more than 150 articles in professional journals.

Paul completed his undergraduate degree at Ohio State University, his master's degree at the University of North Carolina, and his doctorate of education at Harvard University.

In 1991, Paul was honored for his leadership in urban education when he received the Richard R. Green Leadership Award. In 1997, he was awarded an honorary doctorate of education from Duquesne University. The Hope Foundation honored him with the Courageous Leadership Award of 2000. The Horace Mann League presented Paul with the league's 2001 Outstanding Educator Award, citing him as an articulate spokesperson for strong and effective public education. He co-authored *Exploding the Myths* (1993), and he has published *Articles of Faith & Hope for Public Education* (1997) and *Perspectives on American Education* (2004).

A founding partner of the Center for Empowered Leadership, Paul is committed to advocacy for public education and the children it serves. Contact him at Phouston@aasa.org.

Stephen L. Sokolow, a former superintendent of schools, is currently co-authoring a series of books on the spiritual principles of leadership. He is also a founding partner and executive director of the Center for Empowered Leadership.

After working at schools in Pennsylvania and Delaware, Steve served as superintendent of schools in the Upper Freehold Regional school district in Monmouth County, New Jersey, and the Bridgewater-Raritan Regional school district in Somerset County, New Jersey.

Steve completed his undergraduate and master's degrees at Temple University where he also earned a doctorate of education. He was awarded several fellowships and later served in Temple's Department of Educational Leadership as an adjunct professor. He is a past president of Temple University's educational administration doctoral alumni association.

He is also past president of the superintendent's roundtable in Monmouth County, New Jersey. From 1986 through 2001, he participated in Harvard University's summer invitational seminar for superintendents. Steve represented the superintendents of Somerset County, New Jersey, as a member of the New Jersey Association of School Administrators Executive Committee, and served as a member of the New Jersey Governor's Task Force on Education.

In 1986, Steve was selected by the *Executive Educator*, a publication of the National School Boards Association, as one of the top 100 small-district school executives in North America. He was honored for his leadership as a superintendent by the New Jersey Legislature in 1987 and was profiled by the *School Administrator* for his "out-of-the-box thinking" in January 1999.

His feature articles, "Enlightened Leadership" (September 2002) and "Nourishing Our Spirit as Leaders" (November 2005), were published in *The School Administrator*, a national publication of the American Association of School Administrators.

Steve is a child-centered educator committed to empowering enlightened leadership in both the public and private sector, but especially in the field of education. Contact him at Slsokolow@aol.com.

Introduction

As we enter the 21st century, there is a growing interest in the topic of spirituality. The words *spiritual* and *spirituality* are familiar to everyone; they are part of a common vocabulary. Yet, when you ask people what these words mean, you get widely varying responses. Some see these words in a strictly religious context. Others believe they have both religious and nonreligious connotations. Still others believe these concepts stand apart and actually transcend religion itself. We respect each person's right to determine what these words mean on a personal level. Because this is a book dealing with spirituality and leadership, we think it is important for you to know what we mean when we use these words.

Spirituality can be seen in countless ways, but perhaps, it can best be expressed as each human being's personal relationship with the Divine. Spirituality connects you with divine energy. This is an energy that can help you to grow and evolve into better and better versions of yourself. Spirituality can also affect your personal energy field as well as the energy field of our planet and the entire universe. Cumulatively, it is the energy that has the power to transform our world and truly make it better for all of us.

There's much confusion about spirituality. Many people see spirituality and religion as being the same thing. We suggest a different lens, one that uses a metaphor of the pipes. You can have different kinds of pipes: copper pipes, plastic pipes, lead pipes, round pipes, oval pipes, big pipes and small. As we see it, the pipes represent religion in all its various forms, with different specifications to those forms based on theology, history, and practice. Only one substance, however, flows through those pipes, and what flows through is the essence of spirituality. Different religions may call that essence different things. But whether you call it divine intelligence, universal awareness, divine wisdom, conscience, or our moral guidance system, it's still spirituality. The difference between religion and spirituality is the difference between form and substance. What we are talking about is the essence of the personal relationship between you and the Divine, whether you're a Buddhist or a Baptist or a person of any other faith, or even no organized faith at all.

Spirituality is an unseen force that is both part of humankind and at the same time greater than humankind. It's the force through which all people are connected, the great force that no one can completely understand even though most people recognize it in their lives in some form. And it's the connection between us as human beings, the connection between us and Nature, and the connection between us and the Divine, whatever you choose to call the Divine, be it God, or Jesus, or Buddha, or Adonai, or Allah, or Source, or the Universe. And spirituality is also a way of behaving toward each other. It's a way of being human, a blueprint for fulfilling your human potential and the potential for humanity at its best. As you move further away from spirituality, you are at your worst; you are less human, less connected, and less fulfilled. Conversely, as you move toward it, you are more human, more humane, more connected, and more fulfilled.

Throughout this book, depending on context, we refer to *God, the Divine,* or *the Universe.* For the most part, we use these terms interchangeably to mean a higher spiritual power. Likewise, depending on context, we use the terms *higher self, true self, divine spark,* and *soul* to mean the connection everyone has to that higher spiritual power and to life itself. When we use the term Universe with a capital U, we are referring not just to the material universe that is made up of stars, planets, comets, gases, asteroids, galaxies, black holes, dark matter, dark energy, and the like but also to the universe in a spiritual context—a context than transcends time and space, with consciousness and a ubiquitous divine presence.

The spiritual principles of leadership described in this book can increase your effectiveness as a leader if you are attuned to them. These principles are not theoretical; they are both real and practical, and they are accessible to each and every person. The overarching theme of this work is that the expression of these and other spiritual principles of leadership will help you to become a better human being and a better leader.

The Principle of Intention

Almost everything you do starts with an intention, and an intention starts with an idea in your mind. An intention includes not just what you want to do but the why behind what you want to do. For example, as a school leader, I may intend to raise the achievement scores of my students—but why?

- So I'll look good, get a raise, and have my contract renewed?
- So my staff will feel successful and feel good about themselves?
- So I can feel successful as a leader?
- So I can have some evidence that the programs I've initiated actually work?
- So I have some evidence that our students have learned what they need to be successful?

All five of these reasons are possible. All five may actually exist simultaneously. However, each of them is distinguishable by its focus. Notice how in some of these examples you the leader are the focus, whereas in others the focus is outside of yourself and is on teachers or students. Often, if not most of the time, there's more than one underlying reason why people have a particular intention. Human beings are complex, and our underlying motives often comprise a variety of factors that may be of varying importance. Sometimes people don't even ask themselves what their underlying motives are. For important intentions, we suggest that you ask yourself not only what you want to manifest but also why. Ask yourself who is the primary focus—yourself or others? The more your underlying intention focuses on benefiting others, the more you will engender support from the Universe.

Think about something you accomplished that made you feel good, something that was meaningful to you. When you peel the onion to find the inner core of your intention, in all likelihood, you'll find that the focus was something or someone other than yourself. Our satisfaction and sense of fulfillment increase when our intentions are focused on the needs of others. Our sense of purpose and our sense of meaning grow when our underlying motivation is to help others.

In Steve's last superintendency, he worked hard to win passage of a $21 million bond referendum to expand and upgrade the district's high school. He fought tooth and nail to include money for state of the art technology and flexible open-space areas that he believed were indispensable to 21st-century schooling. As part of the intention process, he envisioned students and teachers in an environment designed to maximize their learning. His intention was to have the referendum approved so that the high school could be upgraded and expanded to accommodate increased enrollment. He focused on getting community support to provide the funding for the project. But his passion came from his underlying motivation to ensure that his students and teachers had the facilities and infrastructure they would need to succeed in the years ahead. The "what" was the passage of a referendum, but the "why" was his desire to do something truly important to support future teaching and learning for untold numbers of students and teachers.

Whether or not you realize it, your intentions set up an energy field around themselves. You strengthen that field by what you think and what you envision. You strengthen it by what you write and what you say and by enrolling people through collaborative processes. The more explicit you make your intentions and the more time and energy you give to implementing them, the more you increase the likelihood of seeing your intentions actually manifest in reality. Intention is not only a principle: It is a power, a force. When your intentions are aligned with the higher aspects of yourself, you set the conditions for the Universe to support you in bringing your intentions into physical reality.

Applying the Principle of Intention

- Select something and declare it to be an intention.
- Declare it to yourself.
- Write it down: It is my intention that . . .
- Declare it to others.
- Close your eyes and use visualization to see it in your mind's eye.
- Make note of ways you can use your position to talk about your intention both formally and informally.
- Write more about it and share your writing.
- Privately expand the energy field through prayer.

INTENTION IS A FUNDAMENTAL
PRINCIPLE OF ENLIGHTENED LEADERSHIP

Intention is a framework for the creation of ultimate reality. It's the building plans for reality. Before you can have a plan, you've got to have an intention, the thought of what you want to see happen or where you want to go or what your ultimate goal is. From that beginning, you can start developing plans. Sending the intention out to the Universe creates energy. It creates an energy cycle that is largely outside of your control once you send it out. So you're not just acting from your own center; you're also enlisting the aid of a lot of other seen and unseen powers outside of you, stirring up the pot of energy that the Universe makes available when you create a sense of what you want to do and why you want to do it. You can think of an intention as the ripples of a stone skipping along the surface of a pond. Each time it touches the pond, the stone generates a series of ever-expanding concentric circles, and the sets of circles intersect and overlap at some point. The pattern created by intention is similar to the surface of the pond after the stone passes through, but because the medium is life and not water, the reverberations travel like light and do not lose strength as they contribute to the fabric of life.

Most leaders do not have a strong enough appreciation of the power of intention as a force for shaping reality. People do or want to do so many things that it's not always clear what their intentions are. So it's very important for leaders to have clear in their own mind what their intentions are—not only what they would like to see happen in a particular set of circumstances or in a particular dynamic, but also what motivation lies one step beneath the goal itself. Besides knowing what your goals are in any given set of circumstances, you should, to the extent that it is possible, ask yourself about your primary motivation. This is a personal process between you and your inner or higher self and, perhaps ultimately, the Divine. That internal dialogue about what you want to do and why you want to do it ignites the spark that goes out into the universe as an energy field.

For example, you could have a goal to lose weight, but the intention is to be healthy. The intention is more fundamental than the goal. The intention can even create a set of goals. The goals themselves are not the intention; the intention is underneath the goal and explains why. Why would *you* want to be healthy beyond the fact that everyone does? Your intention to be healthy may tie into your need to have sufficient energy to make a more positive contribution to the world or to meet your professional responsibilities. So intention ties into a more fundamental set of reasons about why you want to do something.

As a leader, the intentions that carry the most force are the ones that will benefit people other than yourself. But that doesn't mean that your intentions can't also benefit you. You can benefit from being healthy, but also by being healthy you are in a better position to serve others. Intention is part of the dance of attunement between you and the Universe. When you're attuned, everybody benefits. When you're out of attunement, no one benefits. And that's a good reason for wanting to be attuned with the Universe because whatever happens for the Universe happens for you, too. There's a mutual interplay between you and the Universe. When your intentions are strictly selfish, the Universe is unlikely to assist you, and consequently, the Universe won't benefit either. So you have to be thoughtful, with some sense of clarity, when you formulate your intentions.

THOUGHT IS MORE IMPORTANT THAN YOU THINK

Why is thought more important than you think? Thought is the "Energizer®️ bunny" for what happens. Like most people, you may assume that what you think is private; it doesn't go anywhere, just rattles inside your head. You figure you can have these thoughts and not have any impact. But the reality is that a thought creates a force of energy that immediately goes beyond your head and out into the world at large. The moment you create thought, you create potential action. It's like taking the genie out of the bottle. Once you think it, it's over. The thought escaped. There's no holding it back. There's no way to think, "Well this is private. It's just between me and my head at this point." No. When you create a thought, that thought immediately leaves your being and goes out into the universe, where it has the potential to start manifesting itself in activities and results.

Believing that thoughts are private, most people assume that they're free to think outlandish things, and maybe even hurtful things, and that thought is a harmless way of mentally processing options and choices. Yet, over our years of work together, we've come to understand that your thoughts function in a number of powerful ways. One is that your thoughts send messages not only to your body but also to your spirit, affecting both. Another is that thought itself sets up energy patterns that you transmit. While we don't understand precisely how this occurs, we are convinced that thoughts can even be picked up by others under certain circumstances and by spiritual forces as well.

It's been reported that more than 80 percent of the people in America believe in the power of prayer, and prayer—whether it is spoken, written, or silent—involves thought. Unless you think that only certain types of thought project out into the Universe and the other ones are contained, you're left with the idea that all your thoughts radiate out. Where do they go? Do they just emanate out like a radio signal that gets fainter and fainter the further it travels? Or are they received and even recorded? There is a mystical school of thought that holds the belief that all thoughts, words, and deeds are recorded in another plane of existence known as the astral realm in something called the Akashic Record. In this view, thoughts not only radiate out but are also stored.

We know of no evidence that supports the existence of the Akashic Record, but the concept of being held accountable, on death, for how you lived your life exists in many religious traditions. If there's no record, what's the mechanism for doing that? The whole notion of being judged at the end of life at least raises the question as to whether people are going to be judged not only by their deeds but by their thoughts as well. Such notions might serve as a motivation to direct thoughts in more positive ways and, because thoughts affect the people who think them, to replace negative thinking (what we colloquially call "stinkin' thinkin'") with fruitful thinking.

Another reason that thought is more important than you think is that if you have one kind of thought pattern and try to act in another way, you create incredible cognitive dissonance. That disruptive pattern between thought and action is easily picked up by those around you. So if you're trying to be one way and you're thinking another way, it's no secret to anybody around you. At a bare minimum, others know that something is in conflict, that what you're trying to create in terms of your outward behavior is at odds with what you are internally. That's on one level. At another level, biblical scripture says, "As a man thinks, so shall he be." From a biblical perspective, it's clear that thinking can create the reality of action. It's very difficult to have impure thoughts and pure action. So you really do have to mind your thoughts pretty carefully.

WHEN THOUGHT BECOMES PRAYER

Because the U.S. Constitution requires separation of church and state, prayer must be a private matter for leaders in the field of public education. Even so, suppose that what people think are just thoughts are in fact prayers, or are at least heard as prayer? Both of us have formalized ways of praying in which we sequentially go through a process of expressing gratitude, seeking guidance, praying for the well-being of others, and so forth. So there's a formalized prayer process that we employ and, considering our very different backgrounds—one of us being Christian and the other Jewish—our processes are quite similar. But thoughts, especially under duress, sometimes just spontaneously slip into the notion of prayer.

Clearly, there are thoughts people intend as prayer and other thoughts that may have a prayerful quality in terms of their content but that people don't think of as praying. For example, you might say to yourself or others, "I wish the world was more at peace" or "I want my friend to be well." Those thoughts have a prayerful quality to them in terms of content, but they differ from formal prayer because the thoughts do not address the Divine or divine forces. When your intention is to pray to a higher power, you have to activate the process in some way. To use a computer, you first have to turn it on. Whatever your conceptual view of the Divine may be, one of the countless ways to turn on the "prayer switch" is to use a salutation to address the Divine, such as "Dear God," "Heavenly Father," "Divine Light of the Universe," and so forth. At other times, you might just use the actual word *pray* or *prayer*. For example, "I pray that my friend will have a quick and complete recovery." In that case, you're not naming the Divine directly, but you are indicating that your thought is a prayer because you state that it is. Either addressing the Divine in some way that is meaningful to you or designating a thought or action as a prayer by using the word *pray* or something like it transforms a thought into a prayer. Of course, countless symbols and spiritual practices turn thoughts into prayers. Essentially, thought becomes prayer when you want it to do so.

If you believe in angels or deities and beings from realms other than physical existence, and if you believe that everything in the universe is connected, then it would seem reasonable for there to be ways to access and even enlist those spiritual forces. This, too, could be considered a form of prayer. You are, in effect, seeking to enlist help from agents of the Divine rather than addressing your prayers directly to the Divine. Clearly, some people engage in rituals specifically designed to enlist particular spiritual entities such as the Archangel Michael, Green Tara, the goddess Kali, particular saints, and so forth. On the other hand, some people address their prayers to no particular entity; their prayer is more like sending an SOS signal "to all the ships at sea," hoping that some spiritual entity will receive it. This is like sending out an open call over the spiritual airwaves to any and all entities that may be sympathetic to the particular concern expressed. The forms of prayer are limitless, but your intention is a critical element in all of them.

SPOKEN AND WRITTEN WORDS ARE KEYS TO MANIFESTING YOUR INTENTION

The spoken word is like an accelerant. It takes thought, and it accelerates it. It's like pouring kerosene on a fire. You could have a fire without the kerosene, but if you pour the kerosene on, it's going to build faster. The spoken word creates a power on top of the power that's already there, in essence by taking your thought from one level to the next level. By speaking out loud, you've upped the ante. You can take it a further step by writing your intention or creating a visual representation of it. There are different ways of bringing energy to an intention, and you can keep escalating the energy by being more and more concrete and more physical.

Support for the power of the spoken word can be found in the Bible and in other religious traditions. In fact, according to the Book of Genesis, the world itself was called into being by the spoken word. "In the beginning was the Word, and the Word was with God." It doesn't say, "God snapped his fingers." It doesn't say, "God drew a picture." It says God spoke, and the world manifested. And while no one can lay claim to knowing the mind of God, you can certainly infer from the biblical story that there must have been an intention to create the world. The Bible says that the actual means used to transform that intention to a level of physical manifestation was the spoken word. Other religious traditions, such as Buddhism, also hold that sound emits an energy vibration that coalesces into physical form. The Bible further says that human beings are made in God's image, which raises the possibility that, as God's children, people may also have the power to create through the spoken word. This happens not in the sense of saying something and having it instantly appear, but rather in the sense that the spoken word sets up energy patterns that help transform intentions into reality.

Thoughts have power. Expressing those thoughts verbally steps up the power. Everyone has intentions, especially leaders who want to change the status quo. So one way of beginning the process of manifesting your intentions is to state them out loud. When you do that, the question becomes, "Who's listening and who's the audience?" When you speak out loud, is it in a closed room or a room full of people? Should you share your intention via radio and television? Should you say it out loud to the Universe metaphysically? You need to have in mind not only what you would like to manifest but also who you want to hear your words to create the opportunity for other people and forces to assist you in manifesting your intentions.

The process of saying things out loud also helps to clarify your thinking and state your intention clearly. When you speak it out loud, you're raising a posse. You're enlisting support and the aid of others, whether you mean to or not, simply by sharing it. You've brought those who hear you into the circle of intention at that point; you've invited them into your place. And, in doing so, you've created the possibility of their helping you. In terms of an energy level, a thought process has a pretty high frequency. When you express a thought in spoken words, you've lowered the frequency and created more reverberation. When you go to the level of the written word, you've lowered the frequency even further because you put your thought into a physical form that can be felt and touched. Everything in the universe is made up of energy, but the energy operates at different frequencies. The spoken word is a different frequency than the thought word, and the written word is a different frequency than the spoken word. Each one vibrates at a lower and lower level. As you turn your thought to spoken and written words, you are creating more potential to bring your intention into reality, simply by creating the vibration field.

That's why leaders benefit not only by stating their intentions but also by writing them down. After writing them down, you need to share what you have written in as many forums as possible. The very act of writing your intention down helps to clarify your thinking. When people react to what you have written, their reactions can help you refine what you are writing so that it better conveys your meaning. At times, when people read what you write, they interpret it in ways you never intended. So having your intention in writing allows you to refine and clarify it so that it becomes crystal clear. Having it in written form makes it easier to share and increases the likelihood that your message will be conveyed as intended.

What Might This Look Like in Practice?

The following are examples of how the spoken word amplifies the written word in reference to program goals and mission statements.

Aiming to keep program goals simple and memorable, Paul used acronyms to convey program goals. In one district, his acronym was called MISSION SUCCESS: Each letter in the word *success* represented a district initiative. In another district, the acronym was STAR POWER, and the letters in *star* stood for the four district initiatives. Further cementing commitment to initiatives, Paul linked each acronym to the district's mission statement. With the STAR POWER initiative, for example, he tied the plan into the metaphor of a star giving off light. When he left that district, his associates named a star after him as a parting gift. This meaningful gift showed that they "got" what he was trying to do.

In Steve's work, he crafted something called the Superintendent's Vision Statement, which laid out his values and guiding principles in eight words and phrases. They were: being child centered, caring, being future oriented, being an exemplary model, quality, continuous improvement, being a learning organization, and lifelong learning. On the same page, each of these guiding principles was expanded into a statement; for example:

XYZ district is a school district that:

- Is child centered, treating each child as a sacred public trust.
- Truly cares about people in general and its students in particular.
- Truly prepares its students for life in the 21st century.
- Serves as a model and positive example for others to follow.
- Continually strives to do things in a way that reflects quality and professionalism.
- Continually strives to improve and better itself.
- Is a learning community.
- Is committed to lifelong learning.

Such a vision statement can be used in orientation programs for new staff and at meetings of the administrative staff to focus attention on how they can use these principles to guide their actions. It should also be included in district publications. Embedded in such statements is a vision of what the district is striving to become, which is an extension of the superintendent's intention.

Having a succinct written statement not only acts as a personal reminder of core values but also provides staff with a unifying credo for the organization.

During each year's orientation, one of Steve's intentions was to begin the process of empowering new staff by focusing on their positive qualities. He used the letters of the grading system: A/B/C/D/E to have them guess their common attributes. The preferred answer was: *A*ble, *B*right, *C*aring, *D*edicated, and *E*nthusiastic. In this case, the written word was used to manifest the intention of creating a positive culture by telling new staff that such attributes represented what the district sought during the hiring process. The very fact that new employees were selected attested to the fact that they shared these qualities, not only with other newcomers but also with those who were already a part of the school district family.

It is not our intention here to imply that having written intentions should be a unilateral process, although it could be. Most strong leaders use collaborative processes when formulating their intentions and then put those intentions in written form.

Suggestions for Action

- Use your position to communicate your intentions.
- Create a strategic vision of what your district can become.
- Create a document that paints a picture of the qualities, attitudes, and skills you want to see in the young people educated in your system.
- Strip away the education-ese that's used in many school documents.
- Use metaphor and stories to move people.

LEADERS MUST ALIGN THEIR ACTIONS AND INTENTIONS

Integrity is about walking your talk, which relates to the alignment between what you do and what you say. Leaders must also have an alignment between their intentions and what they do.

If you have an intention that you're serious about and then behave counter to it, you are certainly undercutting the likelihood of bringing it into reality. At times, most people probably find their intentions inconsistent with their actions. But we have found that when we're in alignment, our intentions tend to manifest themselves very quickly. You, too, can end up seeing some results very, very quickly once you apply your actions to your intention. And so it's again taking it to that next level by saying, "All right, I've got this intention. Now I'm going to act on this intention to make it happen." A lot of effective motivational programs operate from the principle of creating your intentions and then acting on them—and keep acting on them in a consistent manner to make them happen. The fact is if you follow that technique, it's very powerful.

The acting consists of speaking, writing, and doing. Once you have your intentions clear and your potential actions employing those three elements aligned with your intention, then you have increased the power in a way that really increases the likelihood you will manifest your intention. There's certainly no guarantee, but when your speaking, writing, and doing is aligned with your intention, you increase the probability of transforming your intentions into something real.

This happens in part because other people are in a position to observe what you say, write, and do in relation to your professed intentions. The more consistent you are and the more resolve you show, the more others can determine the extent to which they identify with and support your stated intentions. When your intentions are honorable and focused on the common good, you tend to increase your ability to attract allies and resources that can assist you in the process of moving forward.

What Might This Look Like in Practice?

Paul's staff once called him on something they felt he had done in violation of the values he was trying to create in his organization. He could have argued with them about it but instead chose to accept their feedback. He said, "If I stepped over the line with our values, then I was wrong and that's not what I'm trying to create in this organization. Thank you for bringing it to my attention, and I apologize for it happening." It had a cathartic effect with some of the people because it allowed them to say, "Well, OK, he took responsibility for that." By having some way of checking his actions against his words, he was able to move the organization a step forward.

During one superintendency, Paul brought in a consultant who trusted him enough to tell him the truth and what he needed to hear—not what people wanted him to hear—and to identify areas where he might be making mistakes or sending the wrong message. Leaders have to create mechanisms in their organization that allow truth to be told because people sometimes see themselves not as others see them but rather as they'd like to be seen. You may have an idealized version of who you are and what you're about. When you look in the mirror, you may see all the good parts and ignore the bad parts. So how do you get a true picture of yourself? And how do you get a picture of when you're veering off course? If you can't afford to bring someone in from the outside, you can develop trusting relationships with certain people in the organization who will be straight and level with you. You must find people who know that their relationship with you is not predicated on them telling you what you want to hear, people who can tell you what you need to hear and help you see what you may be missing.

One thing Paul did when he was fresh on the job as superintendent was to talk to *everyone* in the district. He found the reaction of the staff members interesting. They would say, "Why are you listening to so and so? Everybody knows he's not going to tell you the truth." His response was, "Everybody but me knows that. And I won't know that until I've heard from everybody out there, and then I'll have a pretty good idea of who's telling the truth and who isn't and who I can count on in the future to tell me the truth." Only by listening and being open to everyone was he able to sort that out. And sure enough, as he was listening to people, he realized that some people were just telling him what they thought he wanted to hear. Others were very up front and said, "I hope this doesn't offend you, but this is what I think you should know." As strange as it sounds, leaders have to value bad news. If you don't handle bad news graciously, soon you will not get bad news. And it's only by getting the bad news that you really know how you're doing. Only then can you adjust your actions to reflect your intentions.

Another approach Steve has used is to state his intention in an area that involved his own growth and evolution as a leader. For example, he had a discussion with his administrative team about the issue of balancing people's needs in an organization with organizational needs. His intention was that those two dynamics should be balanced, but his actions showed that they weren't. He had a tendency to think about organizational needs before thinking about the needs of people in the organization. Even though he wanted to have a better balance between those two ways of leading, there were times when he was out of balance. So he said to his administrative team, "Now that you know that I want to be more balanced, I'm inviting you to watch me and to give me feedback as to how I'm doing." It was an open declaration, inviting them to supervise him in this particular intention of his. He wanted their feedback to let him know if he was doing better or if he still wasn't getting it right. With their feedback, he was better able to align his action with his intention.

Suggestions for Action

- Create a cadre of truth tellers within your organization who are comfortable enough with you to say, "You're not walking your talk. Here's where your actions and words are out of alignment."
- Engage in reflective practices such as keeping a journal and then, after some time passes, reread it to see what insights you get that you didn't get at the time it happened.
- Teach higher education classes, which force you to be reflective about the actions you're taking.
- Mentor someone who wants to move up in the profession and allow that person to ask you questions about why you do what you do.
- Create an atmosphere where supervision is mutual and have your staff supervise you.

ENLISTING SPIRITUAL AND NONSPIRITUAL FORCES TO MANIFEST YOUR INTENTIONS

Leaders would all like to manifest their intentions. Given the obstacles they must overcome, heaven knows leaders can use all the help they can get. By speaking about your intentions and sharing them with the world at large, you can consciously and unconsciously enlist spiritual and nonspiritual forces as allies. You can also enlist spiritual forces directly through prayer or meditation or whatever you might do to put yourself in touch with higher powers. For the nonspiritual forces—in other words, other people—the key is to create an understanding on their part of where you're trying to go. There's something magnetic about powerful intention. People are drawn to it. People who really know where they're trying to go will draw folks to them, whereas people who are confused about where they're trying to go are not terribly magnetic. So there is something to be said for the people who have clarity in their sense of where they want to go because they're able to draw support and people toward what they're trying to make happen. When you talk about enlightened leadership, that's really what it's all about. It's drawing folks toward a vision or a dream. Essentially, intention is about creating dreams and possibilities that you want to see manifest in physical reality.

If your intent is clear, that in and of itself becomes an attractor. It's as though the intention sets up an energy field that serves as an attractor to other forces and energies. With respect to spiritual forces, you must first decide if you believe in them. If you don't, you can just focus on the nonspiritual forces. But if you are open to the notion that there are spiritual forces, consider that there are two types: internal and external. People call internal spiritual forces their soul, their higher self, their spirit, or their divine spark; if you believe in them, then you would certainly be interested in enlisting them. Furthermore, if you believe that those internal forces are connected to forces outside of yourself, such as God, angels, archangels, deities, and so forth, you may choose to enlist those as well. Unless it's contrary to your beliefs, it's good to remain open to the possibility that there are spiritual forces in the universe that can be enlisted to help manifest your intentions. In our own lives, we not only have felt comfortable enlisting spiritual forces personally but also have found it very beneficial to do so.

People believe in a wide range of spiritual entities, including those that can be harmful as well as those that can be helpful. This is why it is so important to be clear about your intention. There's power in clarity—there's so little of it in the world at large. A lot of the world's pretty murky. So when you have a sense of clarity about things and you can communicate it to other people and you can create that communication in yourself in terms of where you want to go, it acts as an attractor for people because they see the clarity in what you say. So a lot of the intention has to do with creating a sense of clarity about what is important and what is not important. We have been far more powerful in the times when we've had a sense of clarity about what we wished to see happen as opposed to having a sense of confusion or uncertainty about it. When you're unclear, you're sort of all over the place; when you're clear, you've almost got a path. As the mystical golfing caddy Bagger Vance put it, "It's seeing the field." It's knowing your destination and the path to it. When you have that, not only do you have the power, but circumstances align themselves around you to enhance that power as well.

What Might This Look Like in Practice?

Enlisting forces on behalf of your intentions has to do with putting them out publicly. By doing that, you create an atmosphere where connections can be made to what you're trying to achieve on a practical level. People come up to you and say, "Oh, by the way, that thing you were talking about the other day, I was talking to so and so and I think they've got a program that would fit into that." And so you end up with connections. Try suggesting to your colleagues, "Here's what we're trying to create," and then see how people approach you with supporting ideas; for example: "I was at a meeting last week about that, and I think that's what you were talking about. I think this would be a good person to come in and talk to our members about this." So there's a very practical aspect of connection making that comes from putting things out publicly.

On a more spiritual level there is that sense of energy, of putting out energy into the Universe, which then brings additional energy back to you. You have to be open to the fact that the universe is fundamentally an exchange of energy. Science tells us energy can be neither created nor destroyed; it can only be transformed. The idea of transforming energy works with organizations and with people as well. When you take energy at one level and put it out, it can change form to another level—for example, it can move from word to action. That's one of the transformations of energy. Think about the way the world interacts: When you put out hostility, you get hostility back, not love. When you put out love, on the other hand, you rarely get hostility back. When a dog wags its tail, it tends to find the other dog wagging its tail. So when you put out certain behaviors and emotions, you will get in kind back. Part of the energy exchange and flow is just that. So leaders have to be aware of what they are putting out.

At a spiritual level, you reap whatever you sow. As long as humans have been around, that concept has survived, and it certainly is true for organizations. If you put a lot of fear into your organization, you are going to get a response in terms of how people behave. If you put out a lot of trust in the organization, you will get a lot of trusting behavior back. It's an iteration. Life is one long iteration of these things. So part of what leaders have to do is to create the first step of that iteration to move the energy where they

Suggestions for Action

- Identify an intention you would like to manifest.
- Visualize it.
- Speak about it privately and publicly.
- Write about it and share your writing.
- Model it.
- Meditate on it.
- Pray about it.

want it to go. Furthermore, once you have an intention, such as creating a more trusting, or caring, or forgiving, or compassionate organization, then by modeling what you espouse and by using the written and spoken word, you can set in motion related energy patterns that spiral and grow within your organization.

USING YOUR "THIRD EYE" TO MANIFEST INTENTIONS

Your "third eye" is sometimes called the mind's eye. It's what you have in the back of your mind as you are living your lives day by day. For example, if you have an intention to create a collaborative environment for your staff, then as you look at events that come your way, you apply an additional lens, a lens that comes from that third eye to see in any given situation how you can use that circumstance to move your intention forward. The third eye is a lens that functions like a sixth sense that's available to you when you're trying to manifest a particular intention. And so leaders are always looking at the landscape, looking at the things that are coming toward them and the things that they create not only to see what's happening but also to determine how the situation could be used in manifesting a particular intention. It's another way of saying, "How do you hold the vision of your intention in the background of your consciousness as you're carrying out your responsibilities as a leader?"

The third eye is related to the whole notion of foreground and background. Foreground only has meaning if there is a background. To some extent the third eye creates that bigger frame. It fills in those background spaces to allow what you're conscious of to have more sharpness. It allows what you're seeing to stick out because it has something to stick out from. Your third eye is also your intuitive sense, a sort of knowing without knowing how you know. When you have that enlisted along with the more conscious knowing that goes with overt attention, that's a pretty powerful combination. Then you've got what you know and what you've thought about in a formal overt way operating, but within the context of something that is coming to you from a broader, deeper perspective that you may not fully understand.

What's wonderful about the third eye is that it sees in two directions, both inwardly and outwardly. It can see inwardly in terms of intuition and insight that come from divine sources, but it is also there seeing events and circumstances in light of your goals and intentions. Whenever the foreground presents you with the opportunity to shape events and move them in the direction of what you see in the background of your mind, you're using your third eye to do that. This ongoing process helps to manifest your intentions.

It's the difference between a window and a mirror to some extent. A window allows you to see in both directions—you can look out or you can look in through a window. In a mirror, you can see only what is reflected back at you. You don't get the full flavor of what's possible. When people operate in the conscious world, they tend to operate often with mirrors because they have created these blind spots that only allow them to see one way. But when you operate on a higher plane, one that's more open to this other part of you involving your third eye, then the light goes in both directions.

LEADERS USE ATTENTION TO FOCUS THE LENS OF INTENTION

Marshall McLuhan said, "The medium is the message." So the attention is the intention. It's hard to have one without the other, if you think about it. It would be hard to have intention without attention, and it would be hard to have attention without intention. It could be argued that it's useless to have one without the other. They go hand and hand, or perhaps hand in glove might be a better way of putting it.

Intention and attention are two related forces that are both powerful. These forces complement each other, and either one can start the process. If you form an intention, you can use your attention to help manifest it. On the other hand, your attention may allow you to see a pattern, which then triggers the formation of an intention to do something about the pattern you have observed. Once you have an intention, there are many approaches that can help you manifest it in physical reality. Earlier we suggested using your thought processes, using writing, using the spoken word, enlisting people, enlisting other organizations, enlisting spiritual forces, and so forth. One of the ways of enlisting these other forces is through your attention. When you give an intention more of your time and more airtime by using your position to promote it, you're giving it more of your energy; you are highlighting it, shining a light on it and toward it. Picture an image from an earlier time of the town crier, who would walk through the town shouting out the news as people gathered around and listened. The town crier had the intention of bringing the news, but it was the sound of his bellowing voice that got people to focus their attention on it.

You've got to pay attention to get the intention going. Attention allows you to gather up that which is important and use it in a way that manifests something. You've got to gather the seed and put the seed in the basket before you sow. Attention is gathering the seeds, putting them in the basket, and planting them whereas manifested intention is the sowing of the fruit. If you can't get some attention going, it's very difficult to get the intention flowing.

So your intention starts as an idea or a feeling, or perhaps some combination of the two. It is something you want to see happen or come about in a way that is tangible. The many ways you have of attracting energy and giving energy to your intention all can be considered forms of attention. And you can increase the likelihood of manifesting your intention by increasing the attention you yourselves bring to it as well as the attention you engender in others.

What Might This Look Like in Practice?

There's a biblical quote, "Where your treasure is, there will your heart be also." The idea is that whatever you put your mind and your energy toward is what you are valuing. Everyone knows examples of people who put a lot of attention on making money or gaining power or, in organizations, on getting the upper hand in adherence to a personal value system and desires. You can be sure that if that's where you're putting your attention, you're going to create a response around that.

Jim Collins, in his best selling book, *Good to Great,* describes Level Five executives as people who put their focus on the good of the organization. There was a made-for-TV movie about Eisenhower leading the allied forces in the D-Day invasion of German-occupied France during World War II. It was a fascinating depiction because Eisenhower was clearly a Level Five leader. Most movies offer few examples of Level Five leaders. Level Four leaders are charismatic and dramatic, whereas Level Five leaders tend not to be charismatic; their focus is on getting the job done, not on enhancing their own ego. Eisenhower was surrounded by a group of Level Four leaders: Montgomery, Patton, De Gaulle, and other people who had big egos and great needs. One scene takes place in the war room where they were planning the invasion. Although he was the supreme allied commander, Eisenhower would walk in and out of the room all the time with little notice. One day, he brought De Gaulle in, and De Gaulle just stood there. Finally, Eisenhower saw what was happening and called out, "A superior officer on deck." Everybody came to attention. Then De Gaulle relaxed because the officers had given him their attention, whereas Eisenhower—who clearly outranked everybody—didn't care about any of that. For him, it was about getting the job done. It was about putting the focus on what he was trying to create and keeping it centered on the good of the organization, as opposed to the goals that focused on him. By putting your attention on the organization and other people, you

Suggestions for Action

- Watch what you're paying attention to, for others are going to pay attention to the same things.
- Track how you are spending your time by keeping a log or a journal.
- Show your attention by what you talk about.
- Show your attention by the kinds of questions you ask.
- Show your attention by what you are enthusiastic about.
- Show your attention through your nonverbal behavior such as smiling and patting people on the back.
- Do these things in a way that's not manipulative.
- Do these things in a way that reinforces that which you are trying to create.

create one set of outcomes; giving your attention to your own situation will produce different results. The critical element is who or what is the focus—yourself or the organization and others.

LEADERS FOCUS ENERGY TO MANIFEST THEIR INTENTIONS

Everybody has intentions, but a lot of them are petty intentions. They just don't amount to very much because people don't invest in them. You've probably heard, "I intend to be rich." To which we say, "OK, what do you intend to do about it? What's the plan here? Where are you going with this?" You might hear in response, "Well, I'm just sort of intending. You know, I'm buying lottery tickets." A lot of people buy the lottery tickets of life hoping that will get them where they want to go. But unless you follow up on your intentions by acting on them, you're not going anywhere.

Steve has a wealthy friend who believes most people don't really want to be wealthy. He said, "Sure, everybody wants to be wealthy, if wishing could make it so," as in, "I wish I will wake up wealthy tomorrow by winning the lottery or receiving an inheritance." But like this man, many wealthy people not only work long hours at an extremely intense pace, including most weekends, to acquire their wealth, but also take substantive risks, and this requires another level of commitment. "There's a price to be paid, and most people aren't willing to pay that price," Steve's friend said. In other words, there must be a complete alignment between your intention and your actions over time.

Leaders have an arsenal of energy available to them to manifest their intention. They can allocate resources such as time, money, and people. They can use their relationships and connections inside and outside of their organizations, as well as the things we've already mentioned, from creating working groups and establishing priorities to prayer. Leaders who seriously want to manifest a particular intention need to keep focusing on it over a sustained period of time and use their creativity to move toward it with relentless determination at every opportunity. Wishful thinking won't do it, but leaders have the resources to focus their own energy and the energy of others, as well as spiritual energy, to help them manifest their intentions. This is especially true when they are focusing on intentions that serve others and the common good.

Powerful intention has to have commitment attached to it. You may have an intention for something, but you've got to be committed to that intention. That commitment leads to action. You may have an intention of being healthy and losing weight, but if you haven't committed to that by creating an exercise program, an eating program, and so forth, you're not going to see a lot of manifestation of your intention. As Steve's friend said, "Unless you're committed to becoming wealthy, you're probably not going to see it happen." You've got to go beyond, "Wouldn't it be nice." Getting the thought sets the forces of the Universe in motion and creates the possibility of help. Remember the old notion that heaven helps those who help themselves? That means your personal commitment. If you're not committed to making your intention manifest, enlisting everybody else's help in the process, either physically or spiritually, is not going to get you there. So the first step is to make the commitment to the intention yourself. By doing that, and by stating and writing the intention, you're putting it out into the universe to happen. Now you've got a powerful force at work because you have your own energy committed to making it happen, and you have enlisted the help of everything else in the universe to bring it forth as well.

One element of that personal commitment is your personal will. It's the driving force that impels you to manifest your intention. There's also divine intention, which is sometimes referred to as divine will. In her book, *Kabalistic Healing*, Shirley Chambers calls it "life-will." When their personal will is aligned with divine will, people feel empowered and experience a sense of oneness; their ability to manifest their intentions increases dramatically.

What Might This Look Like in Practice?

Leaders have to guard against energy vampires. Some people and situations in organizations will rob you of your energy because, in most organizations, leadership is in a reactive mode as much as it is in a proactive mode. When it's in a reactive mode, you are essentially giving your energy over to the priorities of other people and other situations, as opposed to staying focused in a proactive mode where you are taking your energy and aiming it toward what you want to see happen. One of the keys for leaders is to stay focused by being proactive and staying away from the reactive encounters and reactive mind-sets that often characterize an organization. We know that's particularly true in school districts where the "What are you going to do about it?" syndrome permeates a lot of what happens and where constituents expect the leader to do something about each and every problem.

Another way to focus energy is to avoid upward delegation. There's a wonderful story about people who bring you their monkeys throughout the day. What a good leader should do is pet the monkey, admire the monkey, and feed the monkey, but make sure the monkey leaves with the person who brought it. If you don't, at the end of the day you've got a desk full of monkeys, and you've allowed people to delegate upward, giving all their problems to you. You are left with having to deal with all of those problems as opposed to sending them back into the organization and empowering people to solve their own problems. So focusing energy has a lot to do with how you deal with delegation. By being proactive and delegating in a way that is empowering, you can apply your energy where it is needed most rather than having it dissipated across a spectrum of external demands and expectations.

One of the best ways of being proactive is to think of your time as one of your energy resources. You need to reflect on how you use your time on a given day or week and then look at that in relation to your intentions and ask yourself how much time are you actually spending aligned with manifesting your intentions as opposed to doing other things. If you don't do this, your time will be dissipated, along with your energy. There's a notion that in any organization, the urgent pushes out the important. How do you control your processes, your time, and your energy so that doesn't happen to you? By staying focused on the important and making the urgent wait.

Leaders need to use their energy to leverage the people who will support whatever intention they are trying to manifest rather than letting the energy vampires take their energy and suck it into a black hole. Enlightened leaders choose where they are going to invest their energy, not only in terms of the events or issues they tackle but in terms of people with whom they spend time. By choosing wisely, you increase the likelihood of seeing your intentions actually shape reality.

Suggestions for Action

- Set overarching goals.
- Establish objectives in support of those goals.
- Establish priorities among your objectives.
- Decide what you want to get done in a given time frame.
- Use time management techniques.
- Set priorities for how you will use your time.
- Check your calendar and schedule to see if you're using your time in support of your intentions.

SUMMARY

Leaders in the field of education confront endless challenges and opportunities as they chart the future for their organizations. One of the most powerful tools you have at your disposal is your own intention. Knowing that your intention is a powerful force allows you to focus in ways that will help you translate your ideas into reality and bring about the positive changes you envision.

The Principle
of Attention

How many times have teachers said something like, "Pay attention," or "Are you paying attention?" In the military, people really get serious about it, and say, "Atten-hut, eyes forward, stand erect, stand still, and listen up." Educators know that attention is a key component of learning, but it's much more than that.

Attention is a way of focusing energy—your energy: mental, physical, and emotional—as well as the mental, physical, and emotional energy of others. And if you believe in higher realms of existence, attention is a way of focusing spiritual energy. The central tenet of this principle is: *Where attention goes, energy flows.* If you want something to thrive and grow, pay attention to it. On the other hand, if you want something to wither and diminish, don't pay attention to it; intentionally ignore it.

As with most things, there are exceptions but, as a general rule of thumb, this perspective serves us well.

As leaders, one of the most important choices you make is to decide what you want to pay attention to. In fact, what *you* want to pay attention to often may not be the same as what everybody else wants you to pay attention to.

- You pay attention by what you think about.
- You pay attention by what you talk about and what you ask about.
- You pay attention by what you write about and what you look at.
- You pay attention by what you do.

When leaders pay attention to a person, a situation, or an issue, others start to pay attention to the same things, whether you want them to or not—therefore, you need to be mindful about what you pay attention to. Leaders are like attention magnets.

Try this experiment. The next time you're in a group setting look to the left and raise your eyebrow—see if others in the group follow your gaze. They want to:

- See what you see.
- Hear what you hear.
- Do what you do.

The whole notion of being a role model flows from the principle of attention. If no one paid attention to you, none of what you are modeling would make a difference. It wouldn't be emulated. This principle is more complex than it seems because attention is both conscious and unconscious. For an example of the power of unconscious attention, just look at the way Madison Avenue uses subliminal advertising. In other words, even when people are not aware that they are paying attention, the unconscious mind is absorbing vast quantities of information from what is perceived subliminally.

There is a level of attention that seems to flow naturally from observing the leader, but there's another form of attention leaders create by requiring people to work on something, especially if there are penalties and rewards. For example, is anybody paying attention to the requirements of the president's No Child Left Behind (NCLB) initiative in public education?

The Principle of Attention can be used for good or for ill, which brings us back to the Principle of Intention. We believe that when your attention is aligned with the higher aspects of your being and with your higher purpose, the Universe will try to assist you and support you in many seen and unseen ways. Moreover, increasing the *attention* you give to your *intentions* increases the likelihood they will actually become a reality.

Applying the Principle of Attention

- Select an intention that you want to see happen as a result of giving your attention.
- Set aside time to think about what you want to create.
- Visualize it in your mind's eye as though it were already real.
- Talk about your intention.
- Write about your intention.
- Take actions that show your commitment to your intention.
- Ask the Universe to help you manifest your intention.

ATTENTION IS ONE OF THE KEY PRINCIPLES FOR ENLIGHTENED LEADERS

Someone who wants to be an enlightened leader but who doesn't have a sense of attention is like an absent-minded professor who has all the theory but can't find the way home at night. Attention is the grounding. It's a grounding in the now: being in a place and space in a coterminous way so that you are in the moment and therefore getting what each moment has to offer. Otherwise, you have all of these wonderful thoughts in your head but you're mentally somewhere else; you're not grounded. So attention, in part, is an effort to be attuned to what's happening around you by being grounded in who you are.

Attention is a focusing device. Leaders make a lot of choices, and one of the first choices is where they are going to focus attention. What is it that you are going to attend to with your mind? It is a key principle because you're actually making judgments continually, although sometimes you do it at a subconscious level; it's not as conscious a process as you may think or as you can make it. What is your mind paying attention to in terms of thinking at this moment? What are you doing with your attention in terms of what you want to do? What are you going to attend to during the next hour or this afternoon, or what are you going to attend to before next Thursday?

In addition, there is the whole notion of attention to the larger environment— what is the context? The factors of foreground and background are central to the issue of attention as well. You can narrow your lens and focus your attention on something that's in your immediate foreground. Yet, while you're doing that, your focus is taking place in a context, which is the background, and you're paying attention to that at another level of awareness. So what you are attending to has many aspects to it.

The Bible says that where your treasure is, there is your heart also. What you treasure is where you put your heart. Where your attention is, there too is your soul. What you choose to attend to shows what you value, what's important to you, and where you place your treasure. The choices you make—about what you attend to and where you spend your time, your energy, your resources, your soul—are truly important. If you attend to the wrong things or you are distracted in your attention and really don't have a sense of focus or sense of purpose, you lose your purpose for being. Leaders who have a weak attention span are going to be ineffective because their fragmented and divided attention prevents them from putting their best selves where they need to be.

Many leaders suffer from intermittent attention deficit disorder because the world around them conspires to distract their attention and to rob them of focus and because things come at leaders from all directions. As leaders, you tend to be caught in a whirlwind of activity. Have you ever said to yourself, "I feel like I'm one of those little rats on a wheel right now, and I'm just running, but I'm not going anywhere. I'm just going round and round in a circle."? If you get caught up in the rat race, the rats win because you just don't go anywhere with anything. Everything spins around because you don't have a sense of focus, and you lose your sense of priority. But for enlightened leaders, priorities are not only about what they are going to do at 10 o'clock today; the priorities are about what they are going to do with their lives. That's a foreground/background question. In the foreground, you must decide what you are going to do at 10 o'clock today. In the background is the question of what that has to do with the priorities in your life.

Most people have life priorities; for example: "What am I going to do with my intrinsic gifts?" "What am I going to do with the person that was given to this Earth to do something?" Those are pretty big questions. The question becomes, "How do you use your attention to move those priorities forward?" It's a hard question because leaders, almost by definition, are expected to be looking at the future while analyzing the past and, in doing so, it's easy to miss the present. You miss focusing on where you are in time and space and place, so a lot of your mind is always some other place, focused on next week or next month or next year. Although it's important to plan and to focus on those things, it's also important to be grounded in where you are.

Some leaders have difficulty focusing on the now and focusing on the moment, being aware of and attending to what's happening around them so that, as circumstances change, they can modify what they need to do to get to a particular place next week or next month or next year in the best way. As decisions are being made, it is also important to consider the values incorporated in those decisions to see if they move you closer or further away from where you want to go. It is difficult for leaders to focus on the present, particularly with the world's complexity and the distractions and distortions that diminish a strong sense of attention and focus.

So many things cry out for a leader's attention. It's all the little hands in the classroom being raised, and everyone and everything crying out for the attention of the leader. So at one level, you're responding in a reactive mode to all of the things that are asking for your attention; and then, there are all the things that you want to initiate that don't have little hands raised. Perhaps they are internal hands raising within you that you are trying to pay attention to or that you want to pay attention to. Either way, this creates an ongoing struggle to pay attention to the right things, to the things that are going to have the biggest payoff for the greatest number of people, particularly given the finite energy that you have to expend.

You might call this the tyranny of the urgent. The urgent tends to push out the important. Leaders are constantly surrounded by urgency, and yet enlightened leaders have to focus on the important. There's a real pinch between those two things because what's urgent is not necessarily what's important. Yet, those raised hands, those squeaky wheels, those noisemakers are the ones that create the sense of urgency. You feel you must pick up the ringing phone. Cell phones are everywhere, and that's changed the way people behave. What did people do before they could be interrupted standing in line or driving down the street? How did they spend their time? People have become slaves to all these modern day distractions. John Sealy Brown, the chief scientist at Xerox, said studies show that if you were put in jail 30 years ago and had never seen television or movies in the intervening time, you wouldn't be able to comprehend it now because the images change so rapidly. Watch a commercial and count the number of seconds from one image to the next. It's click, click, click, click. Today's world is an environment that does not allow linear, thoughtful, leisurely processing and discourages riding down the river where you can put your hand in the water and just drift. There's no drifting any more. You're always in white-water. Everything is churning, and everything is moving. It's not surprising that so many leaders are tuned in to that environment of action and reaction, of expectation for immediate reaction. We could write a book about educational leaders and call it: "What are you going to do about it?" Because that's the classic line you get in those leadership roles. People come up to you and say, "What are you going to do about this?" There's a constant demand for action. Leaders must learn that the best way to move forward sometimes is by stepping back. But there is always pressure to move forward; there's this pressure to respond and to act as opposed to stopping and thinking, taking stock, assessing, being thoughtful, and then getting in touch with your core values, getting in touch with your gut, and getting in touch with your intuition before you move forward. In some respects, the world conspires against attention, and that's why thoughtful leadership is so difficult. Attention is one of the principles of enlightened leadership in which the larger environment works against you. The distractions that are built into today's world on a daily basis knock down people's focus and their ability to stay in place, to think, to feel, and to be.

In the 1960s, there was a Broadway musical with the title: *Stop the World, I Want to Get Off.* It was a commentary on the pace of life, which was accelerating seemingly out of control even then. Today, rather than slowing down, the world seems to be spinning faster and faster. There's a Taoist joke that offers a paradoxical perspective to the expectation for action while events are

Suggestions for Action

- Practice shifting your lens of attention by quickly cutting back and forth between foreground and background.
- Don't allow the forces of momentum and inertia to move you in a direction unless that direction makes sense to you and is consistent with your values and goals.
- Look at things from every angle in a holographic way, not as a two-dimensional picture but as a three-dimensional sculpture.

swirling around you like miniature tornadoes: "Don't just do something, stand there." It is so counterintuitive to Western culture to just stand there, and yet it's the standing there—the wait time and the open space in between demand and response—that allow the "doing" to mean something and clarity to emerge. We recognize the dilemma and the challenge but, nonetheless, we see the need to assert more control and attain a more desirable balance between reacting and acting when using the gift of attention.

THE ROLE OF ATTENTION IN THE THINKING OF ENLIGHTENED LEADERS

It has been said that, "As a man thinks, so shall he be." Everything starts with a thought. And so you have to have some sense of order, some sense of focus in your thought processes, to go forward. You can't do before you think. Well, you can. In fact it happens all the time. Some people do that but they tend not to have very good results. You're supposed to look before you leap. It's funny. What do parents say to kids when kids screw up? "What were you thinking? What the hell were you thinking?" That can be said for a lot of adults as well. You've probably had a moment when you said, "What the hell was I thinking?" The answer is you probably weren't. Certainly not with a significant amount of attention to it. You weren't thinking about the ramifications or the outcomes or what you intended to see happen where you had asked yourself, "How does this relate to what I want?"

In addition to not thinking, there are also times when people engage in nonproductive thinking, what we colloquially call "stinkin' thinkin.'" "Stinkin' thinkin'" is the opposite of fruitful thinking. There are times when "stinkin' thinkin'" comes to mind for whatever reason. You have the power to choose what you think about. So you have the option of not dwelling on thoughts of the "stinkin' thinkin'" variety. Worry is a form of attention. What happens when people worry, and how much worrying is appropriate? When is it better to acknowledge a negative possibility but not continue to think about it? Your thoughts set up an energy field, and that field tends to attract like-minded energy. If you think long and hard about something bad happening, you may increase the likelihood of the very thing you're worried about actually occurring. Conversely, if you focus on positive thoughts and focus on things that you really want to see come into reality, you can increase the likelihood of something positive occurring. Many factors contribute to the relationship between positive thought and positive outcomes. The more time you spend thinking about something, the more you can see it from other perspectives and find additional possibilities for bringing those thoughts into reality. Your thought patterns may also open pathways to attract help from other people, from spiritual sources, or even other planes of existence. Many people believe in the existence of angels and other spiritual entities. We don't know if it is possible for angels to tune into our thinking, but suppose they can? And if they can, wouldn't you like to have their help?

If you assume there are angels, how else would you communicate with them? Basically, it is going to be by thought or by word that emanates from thought. Your mind is the potter's wheel of your reality to some extent. You can use it to shape your reality. Positive people put forth positive energies from their thoughts, their worldview, and their inner vision. When you're around such a positive force, you can sense it and feel it. It's contagious. What happens to people who put that energy out is they attract positive energy back. They attract positive people to them; other people want to be around them. On the other hand, people try to avoid people who put out mostly negative thoughts and negative energy because they don't want to be around that. So if you're a leader, how are you going to be more effective? By putting out negative stuff all the time, negative energy, based on the negative ideas that you carry around with you? Or just the opposite? How will you get people to respond positively? How will you make things happen that you want to see happen? What you have internally, what you put out, shapes you and impacts those around you.

The field of neurolinguistic programming ties into this as well, suggesting that your thoughts create certain body behavior. Your body sends signals out to people. It also sends out a signal to you. In one of his workshops, the motivational speaker, Tony Robbins, talked about what it's like when you get up in the morning and you're depressed. He suggested you pay attention to how you are feeling and how your body reflects that. He also suggested that you look at how you walk. If you're feeling bad and down, you'll find your shoulders are slumped, you walk slowly, your head's down, you're not breathing very deeply, and you take on the persona of a depressed person. To help change that, you can modify your body. You can throw your shoulders back, speed up your gait, breathe more deeply, hold your head up; making those physical changes will modify, to some extent, how your thought processes go. On a much more deeply spiritual level, the same kind of thing can happen.

We're talking about the mind-body-spirit connection. When people talk about the mind, they're usually talking about thinking in some form of mental or intellectual processing. There is a special relationship between that and the spirit and physical body. These three aspects of yourself are all interconnected and interdependent, so you can use any one as the entry point for impacting the other two. In a world where everyone is busy, your attention is pulled toward the urgent, but you do have some level of control over your thoughts. There are times while you are driving in a car, or walking from place to place between events, or waiting between meetings when you get an opportunity to think, even if it's for a short period of time. These are opportunities to focus your attention and to think about what you choose to think about. You have the ability to take control of your mind and not to dwell on ideas and images that are counterproductive and not helpful. Watch your thoughts because they do become your actions, and together, your thoughts and actions become your reality.

What Might This Look Like in Practice?

People tend to think of being proactive and reactive as a leadership issue. But how often do you think of being proactive and reactive in terms of the way you use your mind? If you're not careful, you actually wind up spending your mental energy thinking about whatever everybody else wants you to think about. You get a call, whether it's an angry parent or a board member, and whatever the issue is, suddenly that's where your thinking goes. Yet you may be able to do a lot more good for the organization if you take the time to think about what *you* want to think about. On a daily or weekly basis you need to identify proactively what is important to the organization on a short-term and long-term basis and decide what you want to spend your own mental energy processing.

Strange as it may seem, people tend to think that when they're thinking, they're not doing anything. You're doing something when you're in a meeting, or when you're supervising some activity, but if you're just sitting alone in thought, it's almost viewed as though you're "goofing off." Paul actually made a joke about that: He'd be in his office at times staring out of the window, and somebody would walk in; he'd say, "Oh my God, you caught me thinking." We suggest that leaders actually set aside some time in their schedules for thinking. The calendar might read something like: Think about how you can shape the organization to operate more holistically. Or think about how you can shift the culture of the organization in the direction of hope and away from fear. You say to your secretary, "Hold my calls for 30 minutes. I'm not going to meditate, I'm not writing, I'll be thinking."

THE ROLE OF ATTENTION IN THE DOING OF ENLIGHTENED LEADERS

Have you ever walked into something by accident? Perhaps you were mesmerized by a good-looking person and walked into something else because of your 100% distraction. Or maybe, during a midnight trip to the bathroom, you bumped or broke your toe by smacking into the bed, even though you know exactly where it is.

A loss of attention can sometimes have disastrous physical effects. That's how accidents happen. People have car wrecks, fall down, and walk into a pole because they lose attention or focus their attention on the wrong thing. They lose a sense of presence; they lose a sense of being where they are and being in the moment to the point that they do physical damage to themselves. That's at a very basic level. Much more common are the more subtle and less overtly disastrous actions, which sometimes do more long-term damage to other people by doing or saying—or failing to do or say—something because of a lack of attention. Lapses in behavior can carry great consequences for organizations, families, and others members of the community—all caused because someone failed to pay attention.

Leaders are in almost constant motion and spend most of the day doing. You "do" a lot of the day, which is to say you spend a lot of the day doing. Some things you do alone, but frequently, your doing is in the presence of others, who make judgments about what seems to be important to you by what they see you doing. They're assessing what they believe you value by what they see you doing. According to what they see you doing, they may make decision about what, and who, they should consider important and not important. Children are continually watching adults to see what they do. They frequently observe a discrepancy between what is said and what is seen, which gives rise to the adage: "Do as I say and not as I do." Adults watch leaders in much the same way. Leaders do a lot. To what extent are you aware that you are continually making choices about what you do and how you will do it, and that doing itself is a powerful form of attention? People are always talking about doing. "What did you do today?" "I did this, and this, and this," and you recount what you did today. You might also reflect—did it do any good? How did it compare with what I *wanted* to do today? Do I want to do anything differently as a result of what I did today? Do I want to do more of something or less of something as a result of what I did today? Language doesn't lead us to think about doing as a form of paying attention, but it is useful for leaders to be aware that the act of doing is a physical form of attention. All of the things that are true about attention in general at the level of thought or mental level, such as attracting like-energies and synchronistic forces, are also true on the physical level, which is the level of doing.

Suggestions for Action

- Be aware that whatever you do, others start to pay attention to the same thing.
- Because your actions speak much more loudly than anything you can say, act the way you want others to act.
- Invite your staff to give you feedback when they notice that your actions are not aligned with your words.
- Be aware that when others are watching, they are paying attention to what you are doing.
- Demonstrate through your actions what the priorities of the system are.
- Visit schools to show the staff that you are really interested in what they are doing.
- Spend your "doing" time on those things that are going to have the biggest payoff for children and for the professional growth of the staff.
- Think about where to put your attention, select an area, spend more of your time on it, and watch what happens in the organization.

In Western society, there is a hierarchy of activities that puts doing ahead of thinking. If you compare salaries—say, a scientist and an athlete—you can see that somehow doing is valued more than thinking. Steve always cringes when he hears the adage "Those who can, do, those who can't, teach." That's a statement about value because in Western society, doing somehow seems to be more important, and yet doing without thinking is, if not stupid, then mindless. Doing on the physical plane is—or should be—linked to thinking on the mental plane and being on the spiritual plane. These three are connected and pretty hard to separate. People separate them and overemphasize one in relation to the others to their own detriment. You have to dream about climbing a mountain, but you don't climb the mountain by dreaming; you've got to get off the couch and do it. You've got to have the thing in mind; you've got to have the thought about what you are going to do, and then you have to have the will to do it. Thought involves intention, and action and doing involve will. The attention of doing is attention to the will and willingness to step up and move to make things happen. Effective leaders are thinkers and doers, paying attention to both. They're also "be-ers," and it is when these three aspects of thinking, doing, and being are integrated in a harmonious way that leaders are the most powerful.

THE ROLE OF ATTENTION IN THE BEING OF ENLIGHTENED LEADERS

Being, as we're using it here, means being a spiritual being. Some people are described as being mindless or behaving mindlessly. And some people act as though they are soulless. When you don't pay attention to your core values, to your sense of purpose, to your impact on others, and when you lose track of those things, you have stopped paying attention to your being. If you are going to draw a hierarchy at all, being has to be the most important because thinking and doing attached to the wrong sense of being, or to a lack of a sense of being, are either fairly empty or, at times, even dangerous. Some people do a lot and think a lot but are lacking in the being category: They don't really have a sense of clear appropriate purpose. Or, they may have a purpose—destruction. A lot of people have destructive purposes, not only terrorists but, more mundanely, people who have a great disregard for other people. People might be doers, and they can be very bright thinkers, but if they don't have a sense of inner purpose, that inner gyroscope, that internal Global Positioning System, then there's a real problem.

One of the things you need to pay attention to is your being, and a lot of people don't. Your being is fundamentally who you are. How do you pay attention to your being, to the part of you that is a spark of the Divine? When do you pay attention to it? What form does that attention take? Is it what you are listening for and seeing with your senses? Is it paying attention through your intuition? Is it paying attention through your emotions? These are a few of the many ways you can pay attention to your being and become attuned to what your being is saying to you.

Attention to your being is what separates effective leaders from enlightened leaders: You can be an effective leader by doing and thinking, but you won't be an enlightened leader if that's as far as you go. To be an enlightened leader, you've got to be attuned to being, to that third dimension—the dimension that creates depth. Finding that sense of depth allows you to create with a deeper sense of purpose and being. Without that, you can create only a two-dimensional picture, one that has only length and breadth.

In part, your being is animated and activated by paying attention to it. So when you pay attention to who you are, when you pay attention to being fully present, when you pay attention to the wondrous world that you live in and the natural beauty around you, all of this affects your being. And when you pay attention to your being, through intuition, prayer, meditation, insight, introspection, and reflection, it affects the way you see and act in the world. So your attention helps shape your being, and when you pay attention to your being, it helps you pay attention to more of the right things.

What Might This Look Like in Practice?

Paul experiences a sense of being in the desert—taking in its smells, sights, and sounds. He listens to the birds, looks at the colors, the varieties of plant life, and the stark yet incredible beauty of the landscape and of the mountains. One weekend, there was a major forest fire right outside of Tucson. Sitting on a mountain in the desert, Paul watched the smoke roll up and enormous flames shoot into the night sky. He thought it was amazing to be perched so high that he could see what was happening 30 miles away. Despite the peril that the fire represented, he experienced a sense of well-being, tranquility, and connectedness to the Universe. Moments like this feed Paul's soul; in the desert, he is more like his core self. Such moments are one of the endless payoffs for paying attention to your being.

When we speak of the role of attention in your being, we mean in being who you really are: your most authentic self, coming from a place where your passion and your inner belief system reside, expressing who you really are and what you're really about. In one of the interviews Steve had for a position of superintendent, he was told by the board that, of the four finalists, he was the only one who spent a considerable amount of the time talking about children. He thought the board's experience was astonishing. Other candidates talked about budget, staffing, or managerial issues as they answered the board's questions, its members told him. Instead, Steve reflected on the implications of each question for children or for what he and the board might be able to do for kids. It became clear to the board that Steve was all about kids. That's where his head and his heart were and still are because kids are an integral part of his being. Fortunately, that particular board shared Steve's focus on children. Of course, the board might have had a very different orientation; more interested in budgets and efficiency, for example. In his responses to the board, Steve was being who he really was, his true self; he wasn't trying to be what he thought the board might be looking for.

Part of paying attention to your being has to do with aligning your values and your deepest calling as a person with the situation in which you find yourself. You have to find a way as a leader to create this alignment through the attention that you give to your work. It's difficult for an organization to be aligned toward the right set of goals and the right activities if the leader is out of alignment. If you're out of alignment, either because you have your attention on the wrong things or because you're not paying enough attention to the right things, your organization goes out of alignment with you.

Suggestions for Action

- Identify an area where your being is aligned with the situation in which you find yourself.
- Identify an area where the two seem to be misaligned.
- Notice that where there is alignment, energy and power increase.
- Notice that where there's misalignment, there is a lot of energy operating at cross-purposes, and power dissipates.
- Where there is misalignment, think about and act in a way that will bring those elements into alignment.
- Observe what happens.

HOW ENLIGHTENED LEADERS MAXIMIZE TIME ON TASK

There's an old saw that declares, "You don't want to work harder, you want to work smarter." Working smarter is having a sense of priorities. Nearly every time management system, time management book, and time management workshop is built around one simple premise: prioritizing. Now, do leaders do that all the time? Of course not. But when you feel like that little mouse on the treadmill, when you're dizzy from running around and not getting anywhere, you might stop and prioritize. By focusing on your priorities, you may get more done in one day than in the five previous days spent running around. It's one of those truths that people know but typically fail to act on unless they are incredibly self-disciplined, which most of us aren't. But at a greater level, what we are talking about here—from a spiritual dimension in terms of attention—is setting priorities for your life. So it's not just how you are going to spend the morning (although that decision could be a piece of it), it's setting priorities for your life. It's about how you choose to spend your life.

Usually, when people think of time on task, they think primarily about their work life. The whole notion of time on task, however, can apply to anything you choose to do in your 24-hour day, seven-day week; considering time on task allows you to see the possibilities in all of your moments—and to get the most out of each one. Some people seem to get more out of life simply by living it more fully. They savor it, but they also drink life, like some people drink wine. They smell it, they sense the bouquet, they taste it; it's a whole different approach than most people have. People get more out of life by their priorities, their choices, and an attitude that sees time as a precious gift.

You can continually make adjustments—to part of the day or the whole day or a cluster of days—by putting your attention where you will derive the most value for your energy. Some people spend a lot of their energy on things that don't have a great payoff. Taking that same energy or even less energy and applying it elsewhere can produce a bigger and better outcome. The issue of prioritizing is not just about determining the relative importance among possibilities but also about making an assessment: If you spend your time over here, what is the likely impact? If you spend it in a different place or on a different task, what is the likely impact of that? You need to think: Where can I do the most good in the world for the energy expended? How can I leverage my energy?

That's what Paul thought about when his mother was critically ill and dying. It's a commonplace notion that no one who is getting ready to die says, "I wish I'd spent more time on the job." If they have regrets it's about the important things they wish they had chosen to do. In her final days, Paul's mother apologized for the fact that her sickness had complicated his already complicated life. "But mother, that's my gift to you," he told her, and then he realized it was also his gift to himself. Being there and being in that moment with her "doing nothing" was much more important than the thousand other things he might otherwise have been doing.

Suggestions for Action

- Make a list of the core values that define you as a leader.
- Write a statement of what it is you stand for as a leader and as a person.
- Prepare a list of the core principles that will serve as your guiding lights.
- Prepare a list of what aspects of your being are nonnegotiable.
- Ask yourself: How can I become more reflective in my practice?
- Consider keeping a journal or mentoring someone.
- Take the time to regain your sense of direction by occasionally stepping back and assessing what's happening before you move forward.
- Take a longer view of things by stepping back and looking at the trajectory you are creating with your decisions.
- Periodically step back to see how you are doing with your priorities.
- Think about how you can relieve the pressure that you are feeling in certain areas so you can direct your attention where you feel it will have the most impact.

Paul was aware enough to make the right choice while his mother was still alive. A different choice could easily have become a deep regret. Although it was the furthest thing from his mind, Paul became a role model to his friends and staff by showing that his mother's well-being was of paramount importance. The more enlightened and evolved people become, the more their natural inclinations in terms of the choices they make are the right ones.

HOW ENLIGHTENED LEADERS FOCUS POWER AND ENERGY

Let's look at the issue of priorities again. Leaders usually have a number of initiatives or goals that are important to them—things that they want to create or change in some significant way. Sometimes those initiatives come from external sources, but frequently, they come from within. So you have a range of things that you want to initiate, including all of the elements that are needed to support those initiatives. You know that if you initiate something without the proper support, the initiative is unlikely to come to fruition. So the initiative becomes a starting point, and then your attention becomes one of the ingredients for bringing energy to that initiative. The more energy you can bring to an initiative, the more likely it is that the initiative will manifest. Your attention serves almost like an energy magnet that brings in additional energy, which is then added to your own. This is very helpful because generally you can't meet your goals acting alone. You can attract the energy of other people, and, again, if you are open to the idea of spiritual energies, you can also attract such energies to assist you in bringing your initiative to fruition. The same line of thinking applies to issues that you are reacting to or that you want to bring to light. Sometimes the issues present themselves as problems or challenges, which you can turn into new opportunities and initiatives. You accomplish much of what you do by bringing energy to what you want to create at the spiritual, mental, and physical levels.

One of the keys to attention is the ability to simplify. And by that we don't mean being simple-minded. Strip away the extraneous to get at the core of what's important—to get rid of the distractions and focus on the attractions. The simpler the message that leaders have to give others, the more powerful it is. One of the reasons that Jesus was considered such a great spiritual leader, aside from whether you happen to believe he was the son of God or not, had to do with the power of his teaching. And his teaching was extremely simple.

One of the reasons people use metaphor and story in communicating is that the simplicity of metaphor and story is very powerful. As a superintendent, Paul found he was most effective when he was able to simplify tasks for people. You probably know leaders who have these 14 strategic goals with almost as many subgoals. Who can do that? Who even follows that? But if you have two or three fairly simple messages that people grasp, you and they can move mountains. Great companies are successful because they tend to have a clear and simple mission: It's easy for employees to carry forward and easy for customers to understand. So one of the ways leaders focus energy on their initiatives is to make them seem simple enough to implement. When he went from a small district to a large district, Paul found his messages had to become simpler and more focused; in the smaller system, communication was easier because it was more direct. You can use your thinking and attention to ask yourself: What is the essential element here that is important? How can I communicate it clearly and make it easier for others to understand and deal with by reducing its complexity?

You can also focus power by staying the course. In his book, *Good to Great*, Jim Collins talks about the flywheel effect. It takes a lot of energy and effort to get the flywheel around one turn, but if you keep pushing, the second time is a little bit easier, and the third time even easier, and after a while the flywheel starts to create its own momentum. When you stay the course and keep pushing in the direction that you've determined is right, people can see your consistency and commitment. This is especially important in school systems where new programs, new innovations, new initiatives, and new leadership may mean a frequent change of direction. When things are always in a state of flux, people hunker down and don't get very far because they're always waiting for the next wave to roll in. When you can get people to see a constant direction—when they know that what was important last year is important this year and will be important next year, that you're going to stay focused—people start to lose their inhibitions about committing. They are able to step up and move forward because they realize that this focus is not going to go away; they might as well "get with the program." It's that sense of constancy that becomes very important in terms of creating a more potent energy for significant change.

Suggestions for Action

- Focus power on initiatives by focusing and allocating resources.
- Use money as a form of attention.
- Use time as a form of attention.
- View the deployment of people in terms of their collective energy as a form of attention.
- Use collaborative processes to increase synergy.
- Narrow the way people spend their time to what's core and what's most critical.
- Concentrate resources on a select group of initiatives rather than dissipating those resources by tackling too many initiatives.

What Might This Look Like in Practice?

One of the strategies that Steve used to provide constancy of focus was to make his goals for the district cover multiple years. Over a two-, three-, or four-year period, the district would focus on different aspects of each goal, but he would stay the course as a particular goal unfolded. When the goal had been institutionalized, it would drop off of the list, and the district could then take on new initiatives. For example, the first year might focus on planning, the second year on implementation, and the third on evaluation or expansion. There was always a mixture of new initiatives for the staff as well as several initiatives that were in their second or third year of implementation and development. That's a concrete way of helping people focus their attention, stay the course, and see continuity over time; it can be used at a classroom, school, or district level.

HOW ATTENTION SERVES AS A MAGNET FOR ENLISTING OTHERS

People who are focused and have a strong sense of attention exude a sense of power that's extremely attractive to others to follow. Think of successful leaders in history: People have been willing to follow them because the leaders had a strong sense of attention to and focus on what they are about. Attention leads to commitment, and commitment leads to attention; that sense of commitment becomes attractive to people. People tend to be attracted to a sense of passion. When leaders display a dedicated sense of focus, that becomes attractive to people.

Leaders are role models, either by choice or circumstance, so people tend to follow their lead. Most children learned to play the game Follow the Leader, so it's natural to follow the leader even though some people may have other agendas. As in childhood, the game is usually more fun when everyone gets a turn to be the leader, but nonetheless people like to follow a leader. So when a leader creates a following, it is like magnetizing other people in a common cause. When that common cause resonates with other people as being worthy, as something that is perceived as good, and as a worthwhile expenditure of their time and energy, then that magnetic force grows even stronger. As more people are attracted to whatever initiative has become the focus of attention, the number of interested people grows. It is like a crowd forming. What happens is that you want to go over and see what's happening. If what's happening is interesting, and if there's passion, enthusiasm, and commitment involved, people begin to think, "Me too. Maybe there's something that I can contribute to this."

People who exhibit attention display a sense of certainty that attracts followers. Think about a time when you've traveled with a group. In determining where to go, what to see, and what to do first, someone usually emerges who has the strongest sense of attention and certainty. The group gravitates to this decisive personality and trusts that person to lead them.

HOW ENLIGHTENED LEADERS KEEP THEIR FOCUS

Enlightened leaders have many lenses to use to keep their focus and not get distracted. One set of lenses works like blinders on donkeys and horses. Enlightened leaders have excellent peripheral vision, but when it's appropriate, they can put on their blinders. The blinder metaphor is useful because blinders on horses allow them to look forward only. Enlightened leaders are always looking forward, looking for the "promised land," seeking the Holy Grail, looking for the possibility. A part of not being distracted is having a real sense of purpose and keeping that sense of purpose alive all of the time, revisiting it, and recommitting to it on a periodic basis.

Imagine that you can talk to school leaders who have been in their positions for four or five years and ask them, "What were you trying to achieve when you started, and what are you trying to achieve now?" How many of them would have the same sense of purpose about where they wanted to go? If their purpose changed, were they thoughtful about why it changed? Part of avoiding distraction is having a clear sense of purpose because that helps keep the focus. It narrows the field of vision down to a more powerfully enlightened area as opposed to having diffused light spread across a much wider area.

Keeping focus and not getting distracted also relates to being more proactive than reactive. The more reactive you are, the more you tend to feel distracted because something else is always coming into your sphere, and each event becomes a distraction from the previous one. Reaction is a response to someone else's purpose, to a set of conditions someone else created. As a result, when you are always reacting, you can't be proactive. If you want to get frustrated in a hurry, spend all your time reacting. Some of the most frustrating times in your life as a leader will come when you have to react to other people's agendas. You are not doing what you want to do or what you think is important, and the distractions build on each other in a way that doesn't allow for sufficient closure or attention, which tends to cause fragmentation. As a result, effectiveness is diminished.

One person's action is another person's distraction because it doesn't make sense to you. If it's not your purpose and not your program, what's going on makes no sense. How many times have your teachers complained about things that they've had to do in the school system because they don't understand what's being asked of them, because it is somebody else's agenda and they weren't included? They didn't help create the agenda; they don't have any sense of it. Why are kids so distracted? Why don't they pay attention in class? Because it's not their agenda. They've had no hand in constructing the meaning that's being created there. They see it as somebody else's meaning.

Look at the school reform movement. Who is creating the agenda in school reform—the people on the ground or the people up in the clouds? Someone else's agenda becomes a constant distraction because it's their action but your distraction. Part of being a leader is not just setting the agenda, it is negotiating the process and the buy-in for people so that they have a sense of ownership. You might be acting purposefully without distraction, but if you're creating distraction for your followers, you are probably not leading in an enlightened way. So enlightened leadership has to be external as well as internal. You have to be willing to include folks, to draw their attention, and you can do this by using images, symbols, and signs to help people understand the direction and to buy-in to the direction.

HOW ENLIGHTENED LEADERS USE IMAGES TO COMMUNICATE

You'll recall from the Introduction that we reframe the idea of religion and spirituality by using the metaphor of pipes, the pipes being religion and what flows through them being spirituality. Paul uses this metaphor quite successfully with friends who claim to be nonreligious or nonspiritual, and they relate to the idea because pipes are an everyday symbol that doesn't *seem* religious or spiritual to them.

Like Paul, leaders are all, to some degree, master salesmen. You're always selling something. You're trying to get the Eskimos to buy their icebox. How do you do that? How do you sell this stuff? Well, you do it by creating images and visions and symbols and metaphors and stories so that people get it, to say, "Yeah, I can see where I need that icebox now. I can see why, even though it's cold outside, I need that icebox inside so I don't have to step out and get cold myself. If I want a beer from the icebox, I'll have access to it." You create stories for people that allow them to buy in so that your actions are not their distraction.

Psychology and marketing assert that signs and symbols are powerful because they are kind of a shortcut into the psyche. Take the flag, for example, such a powerful symbol that politicians are always metaphorically wrapping themselves in it. The flag, of course, is more than a piece of cloth displaying certain colors and shapes. It evokes in citizens a whole set of beliefs and values and emotions. That one symbol helps bring Americans together in common bond. When leaders identify, create, and use symbols and images that evoke shared values and feelings, they have found a powerful and efficient way to communicate those values and feelings to their various constituencies and to create common bonds with them.

Politicians are always offering the media photo opportunities, or photo-ops, following the notion that a picture is worth a thousand words. A photo-op is a visual story. Several years ago, a newspaper photo showed President George W. Bush strolling among the crosses in the World War II cemetery at Normandy on Memorial Day. Look at all of the symbolism there. With the crosses, he's reinforced his base in America, which is predominantly a Christian country. Of course, Normandy has a powerful symbolic value because it recalls the heroism, sacrifice, and devotion to duty of Americans during World War II, the ultimate giving of life to protect American values, especially freedom and democracy. When he ties all that into the current war that he's waging in Iraq, he's delivering a message that the wars are no different. The photo-op was a smart move politically, and the president's handlers were smart to create that moment for him. There wasn't a secret service man in sight in the pictures or video. You might have thought he was out there by himself, walking through the cemetery. Of course, that wasn't true, but his staff engineered a powerful picture.

Similarly, during the opening ceremony of the Olympics, President Bush walked up the stairs into the stands and sat with the athletes. If you were watching TV, you could see him sitting in the bleachers. He wasn't in some high box looking down at the athletes; he was there right in the middle. Again, he had no visible entourage or phalanx of secret service agents. This was George Bush the man, a proud father there to support and cheer for the sons and daughters of America. Another powerful image.

When people watched Jimmy Carter walk down Pennsylvania Avenue at his inauguration, following the troubled years of the Watergate scandal, they had the sense that the president was once again with the people and not holed up in the White House hiding out from the prosecutors. Politicians are skilled at embodying their messages in symbolism, signs, and imagery.

People in education aren't nearly as good at it; although a few make clever use of symbols and signs, most don't understand their power or how to employ it. Marketing and effective use of the media, by and large, have not been a part of leadership training in American education. But leadership is leadership, and influencing others is influencing others, regardless of what role you happen to play.

Paul calls this being your own "spin doctor," basically creating your own message. Some people may initially object, believing that creating your message is somehow inappropriate. However, how do you expect to lead? Our view is that this is a vehicle for getting the attention of large numbers of people in an efficient and powerful way to enlist them in common cause.

What Might This Look Like in Practice?

There's a lot of truth to the adage that a picture is worth a thousand words. Imagery has an important impact on perception. How many school districts have children at board meetings on a regular basis? How many districts consciously put pictures of children in their publications and put a focus on the work children do? By putting the images and the reality in front of people, you are making a statement.

When Paul moved to Tucson, he learned that the state of Arizona gave each school district a number based on when it was established. The first district in Arizona was Tucson Unified: District 1. People would talk about District 1, but they wouldn't talk about the district as number 1. Although he realized the number was an artifice that might have nothing to do with anything except longevity, one of the things he did was to create "Number 1" pins. He then distributed the pins to people who were helping the district become Number 1 in quality, and these became a particularly cherished and prestigious token. At every board meeting, he'd have the board give out 20 or 30 pins to honor contributors to the educational enterprise. He told his staff that, sooner or later, he hoped everyone would have one of those pins because that would mean everybody was doing something to contribute. Paul used the symbolism of Number 1 to boost people's self-concept about the district, which had experienced hard times and was lacking in self-esteem as an organization. It was his way of trying to turn that around.

Another thing Paul did was to create a motto: "Together for Children." He felt that the district had been focused too much on adults, adult issues, and infighting. By creating a motto that was different from what everybody saw as the reality, he gave them a sense of where they ought to be going. By using the motto "Together for Children," Paul gave people something to focus on that was positive and focused. One of the music teachers in the district wrote a song based on the motto, and the district put it on signs in the schools and on the side of the district's buses for athletic teams and bands.

The current superintendent in Tucson devised a clever way to continue the focus on students. He talked about putting the "S" (for students) back in TUSD (Tucson Unified School District). By taking small, simple things and using them to refocus people's minds in the direction you need to go, you can make reality happen.

When Steve first came to the Upper Freehold Regional School District in the late 1970s, the organization's letterhead had just words. He decided to put the lamp of learning on the letterhead, knowing that it was a positive symbol that people associated with learning. Recently he spoke at a retirement dinner for someone who worked with him for more than 20 years. Although it was 30 years since Steve had changed the letterhead, that same symbol was everywhere, on brochures, banners, pictures, and even the retirement dinner menu. Steve is sure that nobody knows where it came from. At the time he made the change, he just knew intuitively that a system should have a symbol or logo to associate with its name. Later, when one of his schools won the National Blue Ribbon Award for Excellence, he not only got pins for every member of the staff, including the custodians, secretaries, and other support

> ### Suggestions for Action
>
> - Put images of kids engaged in everyday school life in all district publications.
> - Use mottos and slogans to focus people's attention on children.
> - Use symbols to stand for a bigger reality such as excellence or service.
> - Use symbols to get people's attention focused on the right set of things.

staff, but he incorporated the logo of the blue ribbon award into the school's logo and put it on letterhead, banners, and book covers. It was a symbol that reminded people they had worked hard and that together they had achieved a level of excellence that had been recognized nationally.

SUMMARY

You pay attention to get attention paid by others. That's really what it is, an exchange. If you as the leader ever expect to have people pay attention to you—and that means having people move in the directions that you see as appropriate—you can start by paying attention to the little things that matter to people. Then, by paying attention to your thoughts, to your actions, and to your being, and by simplifying your processes and focusing on moral purpose, you will have attention paid to you. Ultimately, that will lead to people following you and creating a desired reality.

The Principle of Unique Gifts and Talents

First, it was fingerprints, then voiceprints and retinal scans, and now DNA shows that each human being is truly unique, a one-of-a-kind original. Yet that uniqueness is not just physical. Minds are unique, and so are spirits. But uniqueness extends even further—each person has unique gifts and talents.

Part of your task in life is to figure out what those gifts and talents are, how to cultivate them, and how to share them. So, first you have to identify your gifts and talents. Then, once you have a sense of what they are, you need to cultivate and develop them. Finally, you need to share them. As leaders, you are challenged not only to live and model that process but also to facilitate that process in others. As leaders in the field of education, you have the opportunity to facilitate the process of identifying, cultivating, and sharing gifts, both for the people with whom you work and for the children you serve. When you do this, it is empowering for all whose lives are touched.

What Might This Look Like in Practice?

In Steve's second year as an assistant superintendent for instruction in Pennsylvania, the scope of his responsibility expanded from Grades 7 through 12 to Grades K through 12.

Emma was an elementary supervisor. She had been ordering supplies, keeping detailed book inventories, and handling other managerial duties. She was planning to retire at the end of the year and seemed to be going through the motions in her responsibilities.

Now that Steve was her new supervisor, Emma came to see him for her marching orders. She asked him what he wanted her to do. He said, "Why don't you get out of this office? Go out into the schools, and you decide how you can best spend your time to do the most good." She said, "Come on, quit kidding: just tell me what to do." That's what she had been used to—waiting for orders and doing whatever her former supervisor had told her to do. In contrast, Steve not only gave her permission to be self-directed, he insisted on it. Based on the stories that she told him about her earlier years, he sensed that she was not only a master teacher but also a gifted teacher of teachers. He stated that he wanted her to use her natural gifts, that he trusted her, and that she should let him know if she ran into any difficulties where she needed his help or support.

Then the magic happened. She began by meeting with new teachers and coaching them. She did demonstration lessons for them and for veteran teachers, then planned and co-taught classes where the classroom came alive. She also elected to work with some of the most difficult students in each school, the ones who had been driving their teachers crazy. She was like a cross between Johnny Appleseed and Florence Nightingale. She helped those in need, students and teachers alike, and sowed seeds of loving kindness and joy wherever she went.

Later in the year, Emma came to see Steve to ask if she could postpone her retirement. Energized by the nature of her new self-directed work, she stayed on a few more years and, when she finally did retire, took a position training new teachers at a nearby college. Under the right circumstances, she found her gift. Under the right circumstances, her gift was cultivated. And, under the right circumstances, she was able to share her gift in a way that made her actions a model for others. Her gift continues to ripple to this day. Her "can do" attitude and her ever-present smile and spirit are still with Steve and all the others whose lives she touched.

Applying the Principle of Our Unique Gifts

- Operate from the premise that all people have unique gifts and talents.
- Be on the lookout for the unique gifts and talents of others.
- Create opportunities for people to demonstrate their unique gifts and talents.
- Take the time to learn what people are good at and what interests them.
- Encourage people to accept responsibilities that will allow their gifts and talents to emerge.
- Give people challenging opportunities.
- Strive to align people's talents with the challenges you give them.
- Empower people by enabling them to use their unique gifts and talents.
- Think of the unique gifts and talents that people have as kindling and wood: Your job is to light the fire so their passion can burn bright.

LEADERS NEED TO BE AWARE THAT
EVERYONE HAS UNIQUE GIFTS AND TALENTS

Leaders have to be open to the view that everyone has talents and gifts, under-standing that those gifts are unique to the individual. Your gifts may not be the same as ours. You look at the world one way, and we may look at the world another way. And none of those ways is necessarily better or worse than the others. They're just different. In our collaboration, we were able to put our two ways of viewing the world together to come up with something new. If each of us had depended solely on our own view, the results would not be nearly as rich or powerful.

This is a lesson Steve began learning in his own life as he grew up with his brother Adam, who couldn't be more different from Steve. The two have differ-ent temperaments and interests. The differences go this far: Steve will stop to pick up a heads-up penny, but Adam will only pick one up that is heads down. Steve sees a bright sunny day, and it lights up his face; he wants to go out and bask in it. Adam sees a stormy day, and it lights up his face; he says, "Let's go out and enjoy the storm." In fact, Steve does go to the park with Adam on stormy days and, of course, they're alone. Nobody else is there because most people don't have a brother who sees the world quite the way Adam sees it. What he shows Steve is that water highlights natural beauty the way rubbing oil brings out the natural beauty in a piece of fine wood. The colors and shades of the leaves are more vivid because the raindrops form interesting patterns on the leaves and branches of the trees. As the rainwater replenishes the lakes and canals where the brothers walk, it forms interesting ripples and patterns on the surface of the water. In winter, when they venture out in the snow during a storm, they have a winter wonderland all to themselves. When they are together, they see Nature in a way that others rarely experience it because part of Adam's uniqueness is to have an appreciation of the natural world in the times that most people find it unpleasant or even ugly.

Growing up with a brother who sees the world through different lenses helped Steve to understand that people can be quite different—and their differ-ences can enrich each other's lives. In turn, his two sons are as different from one another as he is from his brother: One son has powerful intellectual gifts, and the other one has powerful emotional gifts. Learning how to appreciate and interact with a brother who is so different, followed by parenting two children who are so different, helped Steve gain a deep appreciation for differences. He then began to extend that lesson out into the world and realized that many others hadn't learned to appreciate the value of differences.

People tend to seek out others like themselves, missing the benefit of rich, "out-of-the-box" thinking. You may be comfortable with people who are reflec-tions of yourself—mathematics lovers hanging out with kindred spirits for example—but doing so is a counterproductive approach for any group or organization you lead. Your organizations need a diversity of skills, attitudes, and worldviews. Leaders must fight against the natural instinct to seek out people who are too much like themselves.

Generally, people don't have a big problem appreciating different skills and talents in their own children. That seems to be quite natural—even a great thing—in your children, and yet it's hard to apply the same standard in dealing with people who aren't family. Instead of putting that standard aside when dealing with colleagues and others outside the family, it's important to remember that everyone is part of the family of men and women. If difference is good within your immediate family, it's just as good for strangers. That's an interesting word, suggesting that strangers are *strange* because they are different. Being strange is not a positive concept for most people, and yet strangeness and strangers can be wonderfully, wonderfully different.

People also tend to be attracted to people who think the way they do, who process the way they do, and who may even have similar skills and talents. It's harder to appreciate people who process differently, who think differently, who are different. It can be challenging; it may aggravate or even threaten you.

Steve saw how this played out in the relationship between his father, who had a traditional, work-focused orientation, and his brother Adam, a free spirit who wanted to explore the world. In his father's eyes, Steve was the good son, and Adam was the rebel, and it was years before the rift between Adam and his father was healed. Steve's father and his brother, although they held opposing values, had one thing in common: They felt the other was not accepting them.

As a father, Steve had to deal with similar concerns about his son, an artistic, musically inclined adventurer who wasn't motivated to do well academically. Both Steve and his wife are educators. Was their second son rejecting the family's values? The couple felt challenged to appreciate their son's unique gifts. From a detached perspective, Steve saw that his son sprinkled joy in the world wherever he walked. Whenever his son was around, there was more humor, laughter, and joy—what an extraordinary gift that was. His son looked to him for validation, even though he was following a very different path. After some soul searching and growth, Steve came to understand that his son was expressing his true nature, his true self, his spiritual being, and eventually, he was able to show his son that his unique qualities and gifts were appreciated.

As parents or leaders, you, too, may be confronted by people who are much more than a little bit different. Your challenge is to open yourself to their extraordinary value and unique gifts and affirm them. Being different than you is not the same as rejecting you and your values. People are not being different to be difficult; they're being different because that's who they are.

DISCOVERING AND DEVELOPING EVERYONE'S UNIQUE GIFTS AND TALENTS

Middle schools offer a variety of exploratory programs—the theory being that you have to put kids through a lot of different experiences so they can explore many things to see where they might have talents or interests. But as people grow up, they lose sight of the idea that life should be a constant exploration. If you are not willing to try something different, then you're never going to find out what your gifts are.

The most interesting people that we know are people who are constantly on a mission, a quest, to learn new things. What they're saying is, "I may discover other things I'm good at and interested in. I just don't know because I've never tried it." On the other hand, we know other people who just don't want to try anything new because they're happy where they are, and they are stuck in a rut. They have found one or two things they are really good at, and they just keep doing it.

One piece of advice Paul gives to young leaders is never to try to polish the same side twice. If you're good at something, don't keep polishing it. Go polish something else because that way, ultimately, you end up being shiny all over. If you only polish one side, you will have a lot of dull sides left over that you haven't developed. It is a constant struggle to fight against your natural instincts to stay with what you know because you are comfortable doing the things you know you are good at. Most people are much more talented than they will ever know. You may have talents and gifts at a certain level that you just don't ever use, and, at another level, you probably have capacities that you never even tap.

It is important to focus on gifts and talents, both of which are plural. You have more than one gift and more than one talent, and discovering all your inherent gifts and talents is a lifelong journey. At different times in your life—your teenage years, your early adulthood, midlife, or old age—different gifts and talents emerge or come to the fore. Understanding that, you can be alert to clues that you have a talent or a gift in a given area. Life offers an opportunity to discover and cultivate the talents that you have, but the choice of whether or not to do so is yours. It is not ordained that you will discover and cultivate your gifts and talents, just that you will have a real possibility to do so. One of the keys to discovering your talents is through openness to your environment, to what other people are mirroring for you, and to what they see as your gifts and talents.

What Might This Look Like in Practice?

Early in Steve's life, his mother told him he was a natural born teacher. She said, "You're like the Pied Piper. I look out the window, and the little children are following you wherever you go; they are clinging to you, and they want to be with you, and you are obviously not shooing them away. You play with them and seem to be enjoying them. What I see is a natural teacher." That was the first time Steve had ever heard such a notion. Once she said it, he began looking at his life, his experiences in scouting, his experiences in summer camps and in youth groups, and he began to realize that he really was a natural teacher. Teaching was something he not only enjoyed but also found challenging.

When he was 15 and working as a junior counselor at a camp for physically handicapped children, Steve met a camper who, despite his deformed legs and short stumps for arms, wanted to learn to swim. Steve thought, "Wouldn't it be wonderful if I could teach this severely handicapped young boy to swim by propelling himself in the water?"

In the movie *To Kill a Mockingbird*, Gregory Peck said, "Never judge another person until you've stood in their shoes." Steve tried to use that notion in terms of teaching. In the pool, Steve restricted the use of his own arms and legs to see if he could still swim. He learned that if he was wearing a life jacket, he could swim by undulating his body in the water like a dolphin. He learned how you can right yourself if you flip over and become inverted face down in the water. Systematically, he figured out all the things the young boy would have to know in order to swim across the pool and taught the boy how to do them. People who watched thought it was unbelievable. Putting on the boy's life jacket and standing there to ensure the boy's safety, Steve saw the boy flip himself into the pool, right himself, and swim across to the other side. When Steve lifted him out of the water, the boy's face was an expression of pure joy. The experience, which offered self-validation and validation by others, deepened Steve's conviction of his natural teaching gifts.

This story suggests three key ideas. One is being open to others and to seeing others for who they are and what they're capable of, the second is accepting their differences, and the last is feeling empathy, putting yourself in someone's place. To cultivate the gifts of others, you need these; otherwise, you will be imposing yourself on them. There's a big difference between cultivation and imposition. A lot of the battle in education today is over the question of whether to impose education on people or to cultivate it and bring it forth.

Whether you are cultivating your own unique gifts and talents or cultivating the gifts and talents of others, the same principles apply. Parents, family, friends, teachers, colleagues, or even strangers—anyone who observes you as you go about your life—can point out the things you do that seem unusual or special in some way. The mirrors they hold up give you the first insights into your gifts and talents. From that point on, you bear part of the responsibility for cultivating those gifts and talents. More often than not, the world will reward and support your effort. It is hard to help others do this until you have helped yourself. It is hard to cultivate in others what you haven't cultivated in yourself. To help other people develop their unique gifts and talents, you have to be conscious of your own, then operate outward from that place.

In Steve's case, once people began pointing out that he was a natural born teacher, he began to seek out people who he thought were outstanding teachers and use them as his role models and mentors. Sometimes, mentors will find you. When your gifts are in the early stages of promise, teachers, parents, and others can help you cultivate your gifts and talents. Once your gifts and talents are discovered, you need to take personal responsibility for cultivating them by using both internal and external resources.

There is a Zen teaching that when the student is ready, the teacher appears. It's also true that when the teacher is ready, the student appears.

> ### Suggestions for Action
>
> - Be reflective in terms of seeing what you are good at and what works and what doesn't work.
> - Notice what the people in your life are telling you about what you are good at.
> - If you hear from two or three sources that you have a gift in a particular area, be open to looking at it more closely.
> - Be alert for what connects you to your sense of joy.
> - Be alert for what gives you a sense of flow and connection to yourself.
> - Look for opportunities both within and outside of your career to cultivate your interests and talents.

There is an interplay between the student and the teacher that is empowering to both. Everyone learns from others, and everyone gives information and inspiration to others. Whenever you are ready for either role, it will manifest itself.

HOW TO HELP OTHERS CULTIVATE THEIR UNIQUE GIFTS AND TALENTS

Paul barely got out of ninth grade. In his early years, he was not a very good student—in fact, he was classified as an underachiever. In particular, he had a hard time in ninth-grade English—straight D's and D minuses—putting him just above the cutoff line for failure. In his district, you had to pass ninth-grade English to go on to high school, so failure would have had big consequences.

Paul is a holistic learner, and the pieces have to fall into place for him. In high school that happened, and suddenly he was making straight A's. Now he was classified as gifted. He was the same person, which tells you something about the issue of identifying underachievers and the gifted.

Paul had an English teacher in high school named Mrs. Crum. One day after class she said to him, "Have you ever thought about being a writer?" Paul looked at her as if she had lost her mind: After all, he was the guy who barely made it out of ninth-grade English. Nevertheless, she planted a seed. The moment may not have meant much to Mrs. Crum, but, for Paul, it was a pivotal moment. Now, a couple of hundred articles and several books later, he considers himself a writer. Yet, it was that little moment of Mrs. Crum's affirmation that helped him see one of his gifts.

In your life, you may be affirmed by people in the smallest ways, with huge leverage nevertheless. The affirmation itself sometimes can make all the difference in the world. Unfortunately, the converse of that is also true. Denigration or a negative comment to someone, particularly at the wrong moment in their lives, can often make a huge difference in terms of creating a downward spiral for them. At the moment they need to be affirmed, they are not, and this may start self-doubt and a lack of self-confidence.

Leaders need to be constantly aware that these little moments can have tremendous consequences, not only in the business of education but in every aspect of life. In a single moment, one teacher can make all the difference in the world. The difference you can make may have a profound impact with infinite reverberations.

Over the years, Steve has talked to many teachers about how they chose education as their profession. Often their decision grew from the seed of a single remark that someone made to them, usually someone they admired. In particular, Steve remembers asking the president of his teachers' association why she became a teacher. She said that in high school she took a business class so she could be a secretary in an office. Her business teacher asked, "Have you ever thought about becoming a teacher of business education at the high school level?" She had not, but "once my teacher asked me that question, I began thinking that I would like to do that," she told Steve. "I decided to go to college and major in business education. And here I am. I've been doing it for 15 years, and I love it. But up until that moment, I had never given it a thought. My entire life unfolded in a particular direction from a simple question that she asked me."

Everyone has opportunities to help other people discover their unique gifts and qualities, but this is especially true of leaders. Your impact may begin with a question—like the questions asked of Paul and of the president of a teachers' association—or a positive comment about something another person does. Your positive feedback gives that person an insight into their gifts or talents: athletic prowess, art, leadership, conflict resolution, people skills, or anything else. Whether or not the person has been told about this talent before, your remark helps them to see themselves in a new way and may lead them to develop this gift.

The conductor and cellist Pablo Casals has a wonderful quote.

Each second we live is a new and unique moment in the Universe. A moment that never was before and will never be again. And what do we teach our children in school? We teach them that two and two make four and that Paris is the capital of France. We ought to also teach them what they are. We should say to them, "Do you know what you are? You're unique. You're a marvel. In all of the world, there's no other child like you. In the millions of years that have passed, there has never been another child like you. And look at your body. What a wonder it is, your arms, your legs, your hands, your cunning fingers, the way you move. You are capable of anything. You could become a Michelangelo, a Shakespeare, a Beethoven. Yes, you are a marvel." Can you then, when you grow up, harm another who is, like you, a marvel? You must work, we must all work to make this world worthy of its children.

Those powerful words affirm individual uniqueness and also prioritize for adults in education what is important. It is easy to lose sight of that. Being gifted is not about knowing mathematical formulas or the capitals of the world's nations. Giftedness involves your humanity—what you have to offer at the human level. It is important not to get those things mixed up.

Leaders often can see the gifts that others have in the earliest stages of expression, long before they are fully developed. Identifying and figuring out how you can help cultivate the gifts in another person is empowering. It is one of the ways that leaders, especially enlightened leaders, empower other people. Enlightened leaders continually have their radar set to spot the unique gifts and talents of the people in their organization. And once they come up on the radar screen, the first step is acknowledging and affirming those gifts and talents by focusing a spotlight on them. The second step is thinking about the opportunities that you can create for people that will allow them to develop those gifts.

What Might This Look Like in Practice?

Sometimes it means putting people in difficult situations. An assistant superintendent in Tucson had been given a leave of absence to pursue her doctoral work and returned to the district just as Paul became the new superintendent. She expected to return as assistant superintendent in a particular region, with the eventual goal of being an urban superintendent of schools herself. Paul told her the old regional system no longer existed, but he had a job for her as assistant superintendent for business and finance.

"I don't know anything about business and finance," she said, in dismay. Paul said, "Exactly. You want to be an urban superintendent, right? You can count on one hand the number of black superintendents in America who have extensive experience with business and finance. Part of the bigotry found in school systems is we rarely turn the money over to black people." Paul went on, "If you want to be an urban superintendent, you need to fill out your portfolio. You have already polished that regional superintendent's stuff. Work on something you're not good at yet, and you can walk away knowing that, too."

The assistant superintendent was so angry about not returning to the position she expected that, for three or four months, she wouldn't speak to Paul except in professional settings. Finally, one day, she knocked on Paul's door and asked to talk. "I came in to thank you," she said. Paul asked why. She said, "Well, what you did for me, I hated it. I was so mad at you I could spit, but it was the best thing that's ever happened to me. I have learned more in the last three or four months than I had learned in the past three or four years. And I just wanted you to know that I got it and I appreciate it." This person went on to be a successful urban superintendent in other big cities.

We want to draw a distinction between two types of assets that can be cultivated. Hidden assets have to be uncovered by helping people either to find them on their own or to demonstrate them. Paul's assistant superintendent had hidden assets that she had yet to discover. There are also assets of potentiality where the ingredients are there, but the cook hasn't put the ingredients together yet to make the dish. Leaders can create circumstances in which people get a chance to develop these assets further. When you create the proper conditions for people, all sorts of stuff bubbles up that might never have appeared if you didn't create that situation. Sometimes it doesn't work. You may put some people in a situation that is over their head, and they can't or don't rise to the occasion. More often than not, however, our experience has been that people do rise to the occasion.

In Steve's district in the mid 1980s, a chemistry teacher wrote a mini-grant proposal to purchase a Tandy computer so that he could conduct chemistry experiments for his students using the computer to simulate certain chemical reactions. After talking with the teacher about his plan, Steve asked why he didn't craft a proposal for a complete 25-station computer lab. "Write about what the whole science department could do educationally for our students if they had an entire lab of computers to work with," Steve said. The teacher followed Steve's suggestion, creating the first computer lab in

Suggestions for Action

- Demonstrate that you believe in people by giving them opportunities to use their gifts.
- Place people in circumstances where they have to stretch themselves but provide them with a safety net where possible.
- Talk to members of your staff about their hopes and dreams.
- Help the members of your staff move from wishful thinking to fruitful thinking with respect to their hopes and dreams.
- Use an interactive process to help members of your staff bring their hopes and dreams to life.
- Help the members of your staff find and demonstrate their hidden assets.
- Help the members of your staff uncover their assets of potentiality.
- Bring people along by gradually escalating their responsibilities.

the district in the mid 1980s, and he went on to become the district's director of technology. As the years went by, this science teacher learned about the Internet and created one of the first areawide networks in the state, linking thousands of computers. All of this began with a seed from a teacher who wanted one computer for his classroom. The seed blossomed because a leader who saw a bigger picture used that opportunity to cultivate the teacher's gift.

As leaders, you can keep your eyes and ears open, listening and watching for people to express an interest or initiative and then using that to allow assets of potentiality to emerge that go beyond the person's original dream. Our experience has been that when you create the right conditions for people and support them in the realization of their hopes and dreams, magical things can happen.

ENLIGHTENED LEADERS FACILITATE THE SHARING OF UNIQUE GIFTS AND TALENTS

Leaders are a little bit like ringmasters. They bring the show to town, and they separate out events in a way that makes them coherent for people. They direct attention to things. "Now, ladies and gentleman, in Ring 2, we've got the lion tamer. In Ring 3, we've got the jugglers." What you don't want to do is get the jugglers in the lions' cage. You've got a problem when you do that. So part of leadership is about sorting out the pieces, and part of it is getting the spotlight in the right place so people can focus on what is going on in ways that make it coherent for them. Another part of leadership is helping the sharing process by getting everything sorted out; you don't want chaotic sharing. There is a way to blend and sequence things to make them coherent for folks. Leadership is a lot about making sense for people. There are a lot of talents and gifts inherent in any organization and in any situation. How you sort all those out and get them aligned is a part of the leader's role.

One of the things that leaders do is to figure out an appropriate forum to showcase the talents that they see. When the showcase is a good one, then it allows larger and larger audiences to see those talents, to reinforce and to appreciate them. Leaders also provide opportunities for people to be seen in a multidimensional way. Perhaps the principal's secretary has an operatic-quality voice. Finding that out and creating an opportunity for her to share her gift with the school's students is the leader's responsibility, even though her job description doesn't cover sharing her beautiful voice. People have gifts that extend beyond those talents aligned with their responsibilities and positions. Enlightened leaders learn how to discover and cultivate gifts, at least to the point of showcasing them so that others can appreciate the wide range of gifts that people have.

People are always putting boundaries around things. They make judgments about what's more important than something else, and that is a hierarchical way of thinking. They make judgments on appropriateness—for example, that it's not appropriate for the secretary to sing because that's not her job. Now maybe she's not the best opera singer in the world, but there may be a kid in second grade who could be. One of the opportunities of leadership is to remove the boundaries.

Steve once asked members of the staff—not just teachers but custodians, secretaries, bus drivers, everybody who worked for the district—if they had a gift or talent they wanted to share with students. People came forward with the most amazing ideas. For example, the director of maintenance was an expert fly fisherman who wanted to teach students fly-fishing. A guidance counselor worked evenings and weekends as a sportscaster for professional basketball games and introduced students to that world. These are the kind of results you can get simply by asking a question in a way that gives people permission to reveal who they are and what they would be delighted to share. The key is for leaders to give them permission and explicitly encourage the expression.

In one setting where Paul worked, people were trying to create more enrichment opportunities for the kids. They thought mini-courses would work but wondered where they could get the teachers. So they asked the staff what they had to offer and ended up with some unusual and rich activities for kids. The school was enriched by drawing on unused talents that were already in the building. If you make it OK for people to bring more of who they are into the work environment, it enriches not only them but also the environment. It can also help others who see the person displaying gifts, so the person who is displaying their gift gains, the recipients gain, and the observers gain. It's a win-win-win.

Suggestions for Action

- Create synergy and action in your organization by getting people to share their talents with each other.
- Structure opportunities so that successful people can mentor the more inexperienced members of your organization.
- As you put teams of leaders together, select people with complementary gifts.
- Create opportunities for people to tell their stories and share the way they were able to use a particular gift or talent to do something positive.
- Give people tasks that are outside of their comfort zone.
- Allocate resources to spread successful ideas, skills, and programs to ever-widening circles within the organization.
- Brainstorm how ideas that have been successfully piloted or tried in a smaller context can be taken to scale.

HOW ENLIGHTENED LEADERS EXTEND UNIQUE GIFTS AND TALENTS

Basically, you have to share the wealth. When you don't do that, when you fail to share, you put limitations on yourself. On a trip to Africa, Paul noticed that the warthogs, the wildebeests, and the zebras were always together. He asked the naturalist, "What's the deal here? Do they like each other or what?" The naturalist responded, "Well, you see, one has better hearing, one has better smell, and one has better vision. Each has a weakness where the others have strengths, so by being together they combine their natural strengths, and they can protect each other." Paul thought this was a wonderful lesson about the strength of collaboration and diversity.

Everyone has strengths and weaknesses. Besides gifts and talents, people have low points. By working together and by reaching out your hand to someone else in partnership and collaboration, you are able to share your strengths and benefit from theirs; you can also cover up some of your weaknesses when you are in partnership with people who can cover your back.

When you look for partners, look for people who are not only compatible with yourself but also complement you. The better you know your strengths and weaknesses, the easier it is to find people who can complement you. Having complementary strengths is one positive aspect of Steve's relationship with his brother Adam. Steve can learn things from Adam, and vice versa. The synergy from their working together creates better results than either could achieve alone.

That principle applies to many relationships, but think of what leaders can do structurally when they put committees or leadership teams together by selecting people who complement one another. You can assemble teams in which members have differing talents, and you can choose someone with complementary skills to work with on a particular endeavor. By choosing people carefully, the whole they create will be greater than the sum of the parts.

> ## Suggestions for Action
>
> - Participate in networking opportunities.
> - Support networking opportunities for members of your organization.
> - Ask yourself how you can best use your unique talents or gifts through partnering.
> - Ask yourself how your gifts or talents can be shared with others through collaboration.
> - Ask yourself how you can facilitate the sharing of the gifts and talents of others.

HOW UNIQUENESS CONTRIBUTES TO THE TAPESTRY OF LIFE

People have different colors and different textures, the variation among them making a tapestry instead of a chunk of cloth. If you hung a sheet on the wall, it wouldn't be terribly interesting: all the same color, the same size threads. On the other hand, a tapestry, with its variation in color and kinds of thread, can be a work of art.

Paul once visited Tuskegee, Alabama, where George Washington Carver did all his work. Paul was mostly familiar with Carver as a scientist and didn't realize he was also an artist. As Carver went on long walks through the countryside around Tuskegee, he would find things along the road—twine and yarn and string, different types of material that had been cast off, and interesting colors of clay. He would scoop these up and take them home. When he had enough twine and yarn and string, he would weave a tapestry, and when he had enough clay, he would use it to make paints for his water-color pictures.

In his speeches, Paul often tells that story about creative recycling to show what education is about: seeing something precious in something that may appear to be worthless. Finding unique talents may also mean seeing something precious in something that appears to have little value. Sometimes, simply by blending together disparate things, you can come up with a unique work of art. The richness of the differences helps to create the value.

Imagine what a landscape would look like if every tree or flower were exactly the same. Differences create the beauty and power of Nature, and differences create the beauty and power of human beings. But how does your uniqueness contribute to the tapestry of life? It contributes to a larger whole. You play a role in a school or school district, you play a role in a family, and you play a role in the larger community. You express different aspects of yourself in each of those wholes; in each, you are one of the threads that create a picture in that particular context. If you don't think you make a difference, take yourself out of the picture, and you will see a hole in the whole. As a leader, you want to make sure that all of the threads get used, that some aren't just sitting in a pile in the corner where they can't contribute. No threads are discards; every one has a place where it can be used. You may need to be creative in terms of finding the right position or complement or right direction for a particular thread, but by doing so you not only enrich the tapestry, you also make the thread feel pretty good in the process.

You can use other metaphors—a puzzle or a picture—but the essential concept is the same. If the metaphor is a tapestry made up of strands of different types of fabric of varying thickness, and different colors, then each one of us is one of those strands, and the tapestry isn't complete until each strand is woven. In a puzzle, each person is a piece, and the picture isn't complete until each piece finds its place. As for a picture, the image is made up of pixels, and every one is required to complete the image. Choose your metaphor: The message is that each and every person is unique, and until each person's gifts are discovered, cultivated, and used, the whole is incomplete.

HOW THE DIVINE HELPS TO CLARIFY LIFE'S PURPOSE(S)

The Divine clarifies things all the time, but people are too busy to pay attention. So many people are on a quest to deny their own wonderfulness. It is almost as if they've set out with a purpose in life to invalidate the gifts that they were given. And yet, they keep getting signals from the Universe to go forth and develop. Every time the signal comes through, they are on the other line, apparently, because they are not getting it. And yet as outside observers, we look at it, and it is pretty obvious.

You are getting these signals that you've got this talent—look how it has been affirmed in this way and that way—and yet you tend not to pay attention to it. The Divine speaks to you constantly. One of Paul's favorite movies, *Fools Rush In*, is full of signs of love between the characters played by Salma Hayek and Matthew Perry, but they're not seeing them. There are signals everywhere about what you ought to be doing and how you ought to be going about it but, maybe because it isn't convenient or isn't the signal you wanted to hear, you may not pay attention. The Divine presents you not only with the gifts but with the ability to recognize those gifts if you are willing to listen up.

There is a story about a person who is caught in a flood and calls out to God for help. A few minutes later, a floating log shows up, but he lets it go by. The waters continue to rise, and a little while later, a boat comes by. The person in the boat asks him, "Would you like to get in?" and he says, "No, no, no. I'm waiting for God to come and save me." The boat goes off, and the floodwaters continue rising. A helicopter comes, and again, he declines the offer of help, repeating, "God will save me." Finally, the waters rise over his head, and as he is drowning, he says, "God, why didn't you help me?" God says, "I sent you a floating log, a boat, and a helicopter, why didn't you accept the help that I provided?"

The Divine often works in mundane and down-to-earth ways. Like the fellow in the flood, people are often looking for something from the Divine that seems heaven-sent. When the Divine speaks to us, however, he doesn't usually do it through a burning bush or some miraculous intervention. He speaks to us through the quiet voice of other people or events, in effect saying, "Here are your gifts. Here's what you can do. Here's a path open to you. Here's another path open to you. How about this other path?" Sometimes it's hard to accept the obvious.

People by and large do not accept that the Divine works in mysterious ways, which may mean through other people, through circumstances and events, and through synchronicities. Rarely is Divine help powerfully dramatic or other-worldly. You need to use your senses, your feelings, the thoughts that come to you, and the information you gather in a variety of ways, including unusual events, to ask yourself, "Is there a message here for me that will help me understand my purposes, my gifts, my talents?" And if so, then realize that it is time to act.

For certain things, Steve has the rule of three's. When the same message shows up the third time, it's a sign! This phenomenon is called synchronicity, which is another spiritual principal of leadership. The idea has been around for thousands of years, but the Swiss psychiatrist Carl Jung was the first to coin the term. Joseph Jaworski has written an excellent book about it, *Synchronicity: The Inner Path of Leadership.* When the same notion shows up in three different ways or from three different people, take that as a signal that this may be a message that you are supposed to pay attention to. With that as a mind-set, people may say to themselves, "Well, two people told me something and then I saw the same thing in a movie. Or a person mentioned it, I read it in the paper or a magazine, and now I just read the same things in a book." Say to yourself, "Hmmmm, I wonder if this is a meaningful coincidence that may be carrying a message for me."

Then test it out. Explore it. If you just ignore it, the signal will pass you by. Think of the person caught in the flood: If you don't get it after three signals, that advice or opportunity may not come your way again. At the very least, it may be a long while before such assistance is offered and you get another chance like the one you let go by.

What Might This Look Like in Practice?

In his late teens, Paul's father was walking across a field one night and literally felt called by God to preach. He told Paul he heard a voice, and the voice told him he should start preaching the Word. Paul's father ignored it and went on about his business. He had various jobs and, in his thirties, was working in a steel factory in a managerial position. One day he was in the warehouse inspecting something, and a man dropped a load of steel on Paul's father's foot, essentially breaking every bone. He was laid up in the hospital recovering from the accident, and he heard the voice again. He said, it was like hearing, "You didn't pay attention the last time so let me come back one more time and tell you what you need to be doing." That time, he got it. But it literally took having a load of steel dumped on him before he listened.

The fact that repeated messages are sent may be ample proof that God is infinitely patient. People don't like to repeat themselves to others, but somehow they're always trying to make God do it by saying, "I'm not sure that's what you meant. Give me another sign." And He usually does. Or they might say, "That's not the answer I was looking for. Give me another one." When you get a message like this, you should say to yourself, "I may not have been looking for that answer but that's the one I got." You have to be open to the answers you get, not just willing to hear but also understanding that something mundane may open a new door with respect to your life's purpose. You need to pay attention when life talks to you through the opening of certain doors and opportunities and the closing of others.

SUMMARY

Saint Francis of Assisi said, "When you work with your hands, you are a laborer. When you work with your hands and your head, you are a craftsman. If you work with your hands, your head, your heart, and your soul, you are an artist." And so the question for you is to find those things in yourself that allow you to access your heart and your soul in your work. Those are the talents you should pursue in depth, not only for yourself but also for those you lead and serve.

The Principle
of Gratitude

There's an adage we are fond of: *Have an attitude of gratitude.* You can't be too grateful. Gratitude has a real, almost magical power. The key, however, is that it must be real. If it is insincere or pro forma, there is no magical ripple effect.

Leaders get countless opportunities to show gratitude. Heaven knows they ought to be really grateful to the people they work with, for without them leaders literally couldn't accomplish anything. Look at the chain of people and events that have our gratitude for helping us attain the honor of bringing this body of work to you:

- To Professor Lee Olson, Steve's mentor, who first introduced him to the spiritual dimension of leadership.
- To Paul's father, Doran, who first introduced him to the spiritual dimension of life.
- To Richard Simon, who in the mid 1980s served as a high school principal in Steve's school district, for using his contacts at Harvard University to have an invitation extended to Steve to attend the superintendents' summer seminars, where Paul and Steve became friends and laid the foundation for this body of work, and who in 2003 arranged for us to meet his publisher.
- To the Universe for the inspiration we have received in compiling this body of work.

Think about something for which you are grateful—your current job, your family, your home, your education, your health, and so forth. Then trace the chain of events and people who played a role in bringing about whatever it is you are grateful about. How does this process work? First, you become aware that you feel gratitude and are indeed grateful about something. Then you have the opportunity to express that gratitude:

- To yourself
- To the people you are grateful to
- To wider audiences, actually sharing what it is you are grateful for and to whom
- And to life, or the Universe, or to a higher power

Think of all this as seeing with grateful eyes and expressing what you see with a grateful heart.

What Might This Look Like in Practice?

When Steve was superintendent in Monmouth County, New Jersey, every school selected a teacher of the year to be honored at a countywide event. Of course, all such ceremonies are ways of expressing the principle of gratitude. In one school, an English teacher asked her students to write a letter of gratitude to a teacher who had made a real difference in their life.

In a different corner of the county, Steve had recently interviewed a candidate to teach high school history. Although he liked the young woman, he hesitated to hire her because her contract had not been renewed in her previous district. The young woman had a reasonable explanation for the nonrenewal and her references were supportive, but the safe thing for Steve to do was to select another candidate because it is always hard to know if you are getting the complete story.

Then synchronicity intervened. At the awards ceremony, the county superintendent decided to read a few letters from the English teacher's class, where students had been asked to share a story about a teacher who made a difference in their life. One described all the things a young teacher had done to help a struggling student succeed. Although in the reading the teacher was identified only by initials, Steve had a hunch. When he examined the original letter, he learned that the teacher being thanked was, indeed, the candidate for the history position. At that moment, Steve knew he was going to hire her and give her a second chance at her chosen career.

Gratitude is present everywhere in this story. The English teacher asked her students to express gratitude, the letters were read at a ceremony of appreciation, and, of course, the teacher candidate was grateful to be given a second chance at her chosen career. Seven years passed, and the gratitude grew. By then, the school principal was grateful to have this teacher as a member of the faculty. Year in and year out, the teacher's students were grateful for the way she treated them and taught them. The energy of that original student's expression of gratitude on an English assignment continues to produce ripples, even now.

HAVING AN ATTITUDE OF GRATITUDE

People often view gratitude in a range that is too narrow: as something that you feel when someone does something good for you; for example, being grateful for a favor or a gift. The attitude of gratitude, as we see it, is much broader than that. It's a way of looking at life that accepts and is grateful for whatever life brings you—good, bad, or ugly. An attitude of gratitude transcends the specific interchange that might be taking place; it is not simply, "I'm grateful for the gift or I'm grateful for the favor, but I'm also grateful for the hurt; I'm grateful for the negative lesson that you brought me; I'm grateful for this difficult period that I am experiencing because it will help me learn or grow or be stronger." So having an attitude of gratitude is an approach to life that embraces whatever comes.

In life, new ideas and understandings arrive at different times and in different ways. The whole concept of having an attitude of gratitude is something that resonated with Steve in a heartfelt way as soon as he heard it; it became a part of him and his expanded worldview. An attitude of gratitude is one of the lenses that is available to you always, not just at specific times. Sometimes you need to remind yourself gently when the attitude is eluding you. When you are down or things aren't going well, gratitude may seem counterintuitive, but it is vitally needed. When you look at everything through grateful eyes, you will always see events, people, and experiences to be grateful for. To help you remember this, you might consider creating a small sign that says: "Have an attitude of gratitude."

A time when we are especially mindful of our attitude of gratitude is when we engage in prayer. When Paul prays, he always says his prayers of gratitude first. Expressing gratitude for

Suggestions for Action

- Alter your mind-set by looking at your good fortune.
- Remember that you are surrounded by surmountable opportunities.
- Remember that you are in a leadership position that allows you to make a difference.
- Remember that you are in a leadership position that allows you to affect people in positive ways.
- Remember to be grateful for the leadership position you hold.
- Remember you have the opportunity to serve and contribute to the well-being of others.
- Remember to express your gratitude to yourself.
- Remember to express your gratitude to your family and friends.
- Remember to express your gratitude to the people with whom you work.
- If you are a person of faith, remember to express your gratitude to the Divine.

the good things is easy, but expressing gratitude for the bad things is not. Paul believes that even the difficulties and hurts he experiences can help him in some way. He tries to accept the good and the bad with the same attitude, and his mind-set reflects a pervasive attitude of gratitude.

Steve also starts his prayers with expressions of gratitude, but his approach is different. He routinely expresses gratitude about his blessings: family, friends, home, health, education, career, opportunities for service, and so forth. Then he adds an open-ended prayer of gratitude for whatever is happening now: a new friend, the return to health of someone close, a new career opportunity, the birth of a granddaughter, the achievement of a goal, a lesson learned—whatever shows up! Committing his heart and mind to an attitude of gratitude allows him to experience life in a new way. Regardless of what he is doing or thinking or feeling, as he experiences life there's an additional dimension that opens when he remembers to be appreciative and grateful for what is unfolding. It is as though there is a greater depth to the experience. There is a richness that comes from life that just doesn't happen if you don't have that additional dimension. An attitude of gratitude is one of the gateways to life's spiritual dimension.

THE IMPORTANCE OF BEING MINDFUL OF LIFE'S BLESSINGS

Why is it important for anyone to be mindful of life's blessings? First of all, they are the dessert—the syrup on the top of the ice cream sundae, the cherry on top of the syrup. Blessings are the bonuses, the things that add a sense of richness to life. If you don't pay attention to your blessings, you will see a gray picture without the sense of vibrancy that the blessings provide. Part of a leader's role is modeling, and if you are not mindful of blessings, how will anybody in the organization see them? How do you measure progress in an organization? Progress can be seen as a measurement of blessings, of moving from blessing one to blessing two. If you don't have a sense of that, you can't appreciate where you've been. Being mindful of blessings is a way of creating the signposts to show how well you are doing and to create a sense of the richness in the life you want to live.

What Might This Look Like in Practice?

Steve gave his brother Adam a book and wrote on the inside cover that he considered Adam one of the major blessings in his life. Adam asked him what he meant by that. It seemed so self-evident to Steve: "Well, blessings are the things that enrich your life. At one level, perhaps they are the things that help you to be more of who you really are. Blessings can come in the form of people, events, experiences, ideas, inspirations, and physical objects, which somehow make us better." As for his brother, Steve said, "In sharing your insights and wisdom, you help me to become a better version of myself and I'm grateful for that."

Being mindful of your blessings is being mindful of the things that bring out the best in you and that create the opportunity for you to become a better and better version of yourself.

There are gifts that we are given—gifts that are part of who we are—that are blessings. What is a blessing in your life? When Paul asked himself the same question, the answer that came to him was that he is very optimistic. Having that internal viewpoint toward the world has been a wonderful blessing to him; he knows that there are other people who didn't receive that blessing or chose not to take advantage of it, operating as a result outside the constant mind-set of possibility that is natural for him. Invariably, when people raise problems with Paul, his first response is to look for the possibilities that the problems present.

Another personality trait that he considers a blessing is his resilience, which may be a by-product of his optimism. If bad things happen to you, it's a lot easier to bounce back if you are optimistically focused on the knowledge that some good will come of it instead of thinking about how horrible it is and wondering how you are going to get through.

People are given blessings in all of the different dimensions of their lives. You need to be sufficiently attuned to what's happening to step back and say, "That's a blessing. That's something that I should be grateful for." If you asked a room full of people to write down a list of blessings in their lives, given enough time and thought, they would have long lists. Although some common themes would emerge, some blessings would be unique to each person. Sometimes people complain about being taken for granted or not being appreciated. When you are mindful of the abundant blessings in your life, you are less likely to take people, events, and experiences for granted, and you are more likely to appreciate them.

As a child, Paul rarely asked for any specific gifts at Christmas time. He wanted to be surprised. Because he didn't have high expectations, he was rarely disappointed, and he was grateful for whatever he got. He did not have the entitlement mentality prevalent in today's society. Imagine what it would be like if the worldview based on entitlement were replaced with an attitude of gratitude, where people were grateful for the air they breathe, for clean water to drink, for a society where freedom prevails and a country where most people are employed, for the food they eat and good health.

Life always provides things to be grateful for. On a trip to India, Paul saw people living in incredible poverty, some of them sick, yet they had beautiful smiles. They were living a happy life because they loved what they had and the fact that they were alive. That is the baseline from which everything else springs: "I'm grateful to be alive." Gratitude for life itself is an expression of holiness, stemming from an awareness that life itself is holy. Although it may not be a universal view, both of us share it, even though we come from different religious backgrounds.

THE EFFECT OF SHOWING GRATITUDE FOR HELP AND SUPPORT

When you show gratitude for the help and support you receive, the impact just multiplies—the good stuff just keeps coming. Gratitude creates plentitude. You end up with more, and when you are not grateful, you typically end up with less. Lacking gratitude, even those who have much may experience life as empty and sterile because they don't appreciate what they have. Gratitude is a magic word, the "open sesame" of life. When you are grateful and can express gratitude in appropriate terms, the rock rolls away, and the treasure is revealed.

Gratitude begets gratitude. Its expression attracts similar energy in others and in the Universe so that the very act of expressing gratitude sends out an energy field that not only comes back but also is magnified. Think of it as sprinkling Miracle-Gro® in the garden of life. Gratitude has the effect of almost magically creating abundance; you sprinkle it out there and watch everything grow.

People tell little children that the magic words are *please* and *thank you*. They are still magic words even when you grow up. How many notes do you write to people expressing your gratitude? Do you appreciate how important those notes are to people? The words are important. You may *say* thank you, but if you take the next step and put the words in writing, they are even more powerful. You can use e-mail or print a letter off your computer, but the message will mean more if you write a note or letter by hand. Handwriting seems so much stronger than electronic communication because it is more personal. We save expressions of gratitude that we have received, and imagine that you might do so as well.

Paul typically receives notes and letters about speeches he has given or articles he has written. When he gets thank you notes or e-mails from people, it makes him feel like he wants to do more, which is part of that *miracle grow* effect. Gratitude is not just *miracle grow* for what you've already seeded, it's *miracle grow* for the people you are interacting with, too. It reinforces whatever good things you are doing. You want to do more when you know that what you are doing is appreciated and valued. It's not so much that you're looking for the pat on the back; rather, it's gratifying to be told that your energy and effort have meaning for other people. Knowing that, you want to do even more. It's a way of feeding the engine, of refueling.

What Might This Look Like in Practice?

When Paul gave a speech in Arizona, one of his former staff members said, "Come on over—I want you to meet somebody. You probably don't remember her. But she used to wait on your table at the restaurant where she worked when you lived here. Do you remember what you said to her?" Paul responded, "Of course not." His staff member said the woman had told him that "every time you ate there, you asked her why she isn't finishing her teaching degree and going into teaching—and that we needed good teachers. She went back to school, got her degree, and now she's an assistant principal. She remembered that, so she wants to say hello." When Paul met her, she said, "You probably don't remember this but . . ." In fact, Paul did remember her, and the first thing he said was, "You know we need good superintendents, when are you going to go after that?" He continued spreading his *miracle grow* for people, but what he felt was gratitude for having had the opportunity to do that. It put fuel back in his engine. What a gift! As leaders, you all have the gift of being able to spread *miracle grow* on the lives of others.

Leadership in education largely centers on the opportunity for service, a place from which gratitude easily flows. How many people get a chance to make a difference in the lives of other people? How could you not be grateful for that? Ultimately, aren't you grateful for the children you serve? Otherwise, what would you be doing with your life? Every year at springtime, when she'd see all the pregnant women, Steve's wife, Laney, used to say, "There's your future kindergarten class." Steve would think, "I'm sure grateful for that."

THE IMPORTANCE OF BEING GRATEFUL FOR PROGRESS

All of life is incremental. Leaders should seek and try to create transformation, understanding that like most change and improvement, true transformation comes incrementally. At one level, you have to be grateful for a sense of progress because that is your measure of where you've been and how far you have left to go. Measuring progress allows you to know how you are doing. When you get frustrated at work, take a moment to look at how far you've come. Instead of looking forward and talking about where you and your organization haven't gone yet and how far you have to go, just turn around for a second and appreciate the distance from where you started. When you do that, you tend to feel better about yourself, which then empowers you to tackle what is yet to come. It's so easy to take the progress you've made for granted. But when you are reminded of a previous baseline and how far you've come, it helps us see that you can go that far again from today's baseline.

At one time, Paul's board members lacked awareness and appreciation about where they'd come from as an organization; so instead, they were focusing on their present frustrations. Paul realized that he had not followed an old practice, which was make a chart to show where the organization was financially when he came in and where they were at the present time. When he made the chart, the difference wasn't just interesting—it was dramatic. Paul realized then that he had neglected to give his board an important piece of information, and he was penalized for that. The board didn't appreciate the organization's progress because members simply didn't have baseline information.

With all the changes in organizations over time, maintaining an institutional memory becomes more and more difficult. Thus to create a grateful attitude about progress, leaders should be able to benchmark progress from an historical perspective—ignoring people who say, "I only care about where we are today" or "what have you done for me lately?" The reason that Paul stopped reminding people of their progress is that people seemed to be bored by it. He should not have given in to their boredom because the fact is that the ones who were bored were the ones who had been on the board for a while, but there are always new people. Like rivers, organizations are always changing. Just as you never step exactly in the same water twice, people are always coming in who don't have that same sense of history. And unfortunately, because they were not part of the team that helped create the former progress, they don't have the sense of ownership and appreciation that they could or should.

One of the things that former University of Southern California Professor Terry Deal stresses in his writings is the issue of celebration. He says that organizations should celebrate milestones and steps of progress because it empowers people to go forward; it gives you a sense of achievement and completion and satisfaction that you've done something, even while you recognize that you still have more to do. In many organizations—and education is particularly notorious—leaders do very little celebrating; as a profession, educators tend to be overly modest. They somehow feel it is inappropriate to draw attention to themselves, or they don't take credit for what others expected them to do—as though accomplishing it were no big deal.

Some people have the attitude that, "You get paid to do a job—do the job. You get your paycheck and that is the social contract that we have." This narrow view doesn't unleash human potential because, although everyone wants to earn a living, that's not the core value explaining why people work. People are hard-wired to want to make a difference; they're hard-wired

Suggestions for Action

- Look at where you've been to measure where you've come from.
- Ask yourself, "How far have we come since the last time that we looked at this?"
- Ask yourself, "How are we doing compared to where we were a month ago, or a year ago?"
- Keep your focus on moving forward and measure incremental steps to mark your progress.
- Invest in the growth of the organization.
- Invest in the growth of the staff.
- Become a cheerleader by punctuating increments of growth, however small.
- Remember to focus on the journey, not just the bottom line.
- Broaden your view of progress to include progress in terms of the human spirit, progress in term of openness, and progress in terms of creativity.

to want to have progress in their lives. They want to see progress in their own growth and evolution and progress in their organization's growth and evolution. That's what people need to feel valued and gratified. Progress is essential because if things are not living and growing, they're deteriorating and dying. Progress is not just about moving forward, it is about growing and evolving. It is important for leaders to help people understand that.

What Might This Look Like in Practice?

We agree with the old General Electric tagline, "Progress is our most important product." Progress should be something that you measure for yourself, not just something that someone else declares about you. In fact, you are in the best position to know if you have made progress. Paul requires his staff to do self-assessments because he knows that if he assessed them without their input, he would come to a different set of conclusions. Reading their self-assessments is a great revelation to him, showing all the things they did that he had forgotten about or wasn't aware of or had not taken as seriously as they did. Progress has to be driven first and foremost by internal forces, and not just by some external activity. Leadership is about giving a kernel of possibility to people and then giving them the opportunity to measure their own growth as those possibilities blossom.

ENLIGHTENED LEADERS ARE GRATEFUL FOR OBSTACLES AND ADVERSARIES

We subscribe to Nietzsche's reflection that "what doesn't kill you makes you stronger." Most of Paul's greatest progress has come from obstacles, adversity, and adversaries, times when he experienced pain or learned a tough lesson. This may say something about him and his makeup. It is easier to grow from bad lessons than it is from good lessons. People tend to take the good stuff for granted, whereas the bad stuff makes them stop and pay attention. With the good stuff, you move on, continuing in the same direction without thinking too much about it. When things are going poorly, you have to stop and figure out what needs to be changed or added or subtracted to improve the situation.

Paul is proud of the people who are his enemies, and he has tried to choose them well. He is as careful choosing his enemies as choosing his friends because both say much about who you are and what you stand for. If some people didn't oppose him, he would worry about himself. Now Paul is not advocating that you go out of your way to create enemies—although some people do that, alienating everyone around them. But it is a good thing if some people oppose you.

Paul recalls a White House event at which a woman said some negative things about him. He smiled at her, thinking, "If you don't like what I'm saying and doing, I'm probably hitting the right note." Such encounters define who you are in an appropriate way, and you should be grateful for the clarification. They make you stronger, and they can give you lessons that allow you to redo or rethink something—you're not always right. When someone opposes you, it might be because you're wrong, so opposition makes you pause and reflect, a useful tool for leaders. Sometimes you reflect and decide, "No, the opposition is wrong"; you believe you are moving in the right way, and the opposition reinforces your commitment to that direction. Other times, you say, "Wait a minute, there's an interesting point here that I haven't considered. I had better regroup and see what I need to modify and do differently."

What Might This Look Like in Practice?

At night, when Paul says his prayer of gratitude, he includes seemingly negative things. He always tries to remember to be grateful for the tough lesson, for the problems of the moment, and then he asks for guidance to be able to benefit from what he is experiencing in a way that makes him a better person. One of his favorite scenes comes from the movie *Little Big Man*, with Dustin Hoffman playing opposite Old Lodge Skins, an Indian chief who knows he is going to die. The chief offers a prayer of gratitude to the Great Spirit, saying thank you both for his friends and for his enemies because the latter made him stronger. Now blind, Chief Lodge Skins thanks the Great Spirit for his eyesight and for his blindness, which let him see even further. The chief's prayer captures what we are talking about in terms of having gratitude for all things: the good, the bad, and the ugly. The sum total makes you who and what you are. If some of them were missing, you would be much less.

When you encounter major obstacles on the path to your goals, it is a little like mountain climbing. You want to climb the mountain and get to the top, showing that you were able to overcome all the adversarial conditions and obstacles in your way to achieving whatever goal has been set. A number of years ago, Steve had an opportunity to hike the Grand Canyon, which is no walk in the park. It's like mountain climbing in reverse: You start at the top, head toward the bottom, and then climb back up. He remembers the feeling of accomplishment, knowing that he had endured the difficult climb and not given up—about 300 people a year do give up and are taken out by helicopter; a few even die. At the end, Steve was so fatigued that he literally pulled himself over the edge, crawled the last few yards, and collapsed, not having the strength to move another inch until he lay there on the ground and recuperated. Such experiences give you not only a sense of accomplishment but the confidence that you can go up against something difficult and prevail, not only in Nature but in life.

In Steve's professional life, he has encountered countless obstacles and adversaries. During the toughest encounters, he reminds himself of the adage that "whatever doesn't kill you makes you stronger." At the times when he felt more like a warrior than an educator, he relied on a wide range of spiritual principles not only for strength but also for guidance and a sense of direction in the midst of the battles. Leadership is not for the faint of heart. It requires not only physical endurance and stamina but also resilience and inner strength.

Steve's resilience and inner strength were tested almost immediately as a new superintendent in the mid 1970s, when he uncovered a 20 percent short-fall in the revenue side of the school district's budget three months into the school year. To avoid becoming the first school district in the country to close down in April when the funds ran out, Steve persuaded the district's administrators and teachers to take a 10 percent cut in pay for the second half of the school year if, and only if, the community approved additional funding in a special emergency budget election. By 29 votes, the community turned down the request to raise school taxes by 15 percent to resolve the financial crisis. Rather than shut the district down, Steve recommended that the school board appeal to the state commissioner of education to intervene. The commissioner ordered the community to raise taxes not by 15 percent but by 30 percent to resolve the crisis. Steve learned early on that when you are involved in substantially raising people's taxes, adversaries multiply like bees around a jar of honey.

Leaders know that everyone trying to achieve something has obstacles to overcome. As you can rise to meet each occasion, it helps to see the obstacles you encounter not as something to bemoan or complain about but as opportunities to grow and achieve and to feel better about yourself.

Obstacles also give you a measure for gratitude. You can appreciate the climb to the top of the mountain only by standing in the valley, for the valley marks the mountain's height. When you are standing in the bottom of the valley and you look up and see how far it is up there, and then you climb the mountain, you know you've done something. It gives you a sense of what to be grateful for. In the same way, obstacles and difficulties not only allow you to be grateful for the victories but also give your victories the meaning they deserve.

Suggestions for Action

- Remember that "what doesn't kill you makes you stronger."
- Remember that it is the moments of difficulty that define you as a leader.
- Remember that large challenges allow you rise to large heights.
- Remember that great challenges bring out greatness in people.
- Remember that your adversaries allow you to sharpen your tools.
- Remember that your adversaries help you to define who you are in relation to who they are.
- Remember that every obstacle is an opportunity in disguise.
- When confronting obstacles, remember George Bernard Shaw's words, quoted by Bobby Kennedy, "Some people see things as they are and ask why, and I see things that never were, and ask why not?"

SHOWING YOU ARE GRATEFUL FOR LOVE RECEIVED

One of the ways to show you are grateful for love received is by being more loving yourself. One of the Beatles' songs includes the line, "In the end, the love you take is equal to the love you make." You show your gratitude for love, in part, by loving back. You become a more loving person, and in doing so, you show a certain gratitude for what you've received. This doesn't mean that you talk more about love; it means you act in more loving ways, treating *love* as a verb. For some people, being loved takes their rough edges off and rounds them out. Another way to show you are grateful for the love you receive is by trying to be a better person. In the movie *As Good As It Gets,* the character played by Jack Nicholson tells his movie girlfriend, "You make me want to be a better man."

With a broad view of love, which is the ultimate form of caring, you recognize just how much and how often love comes your way. It comes not only *in* many different forms but also *through* many different forms: coworkers or colleagues as well as family or friends, sometimes from our pets, sometimes from divine sources, and, one could argue, sometimes even from life itself. This view gives you a bigger playing field for showing your gratitude.

SHOWING YOU ARE GRATEFUL FOR LOVE ACCEPTED

Some people are comfortable giving love in various measures: They are caring people who try to give of themselves in a loving way to the people around them and the environments in which they live. It takes a different attitude, however, to accept the love that comes to you and not just blow it off, disregard it, or say it makes you uncomfortable or you don't need it. We think it actually may be harder for some people to be gracious in accepting expressions of love than for them to give love.

For leaders, it is especially important to be open to the energy of love that comes their way. With love, it may be more blessed to receive than to give because, ultimately, it is only by receiving that you have it to give. If you can't accept love, it becomes much harder, if not impossible, to give it. If you are open to receiving love, it is just like gratitude; the more you get, the more you have to give, and the more you want to give.

One reason many people find it hard to receive or accept love is that they may feel unworthy at some level. Remember the old Woody Allen line, "How could I be a part of a club that would have me as a member?" Or, in other words, how could I possibly get involved with you if you were willing to love me, since I'm not worthy of being loved? In other cases, people are just uncomfortable with love. They don't know how to handle it, and so they feel awkward, lacking the grace to know how to accept it. Although the inability to accept love may be widespread, it is especially problematic for leaders. By virtue of your position, you may receive love from those that you lead. If you can't be grateful for that and accept it, your ability to lead may be restricted because you don't reciprocate appropriately.

Being grateful for love received presumes you are willing to acknowledge receiving it, but many people don't or won't. Some may be afraid to show that they like receiving love because they might become dependent on it, and how can you be sure it will be there when you want it? Will it hurt, if for some reason it stops?

Accepting love also empowers the giver. If you accept the love that others bestow on you, and they can see that, it empowers them. Acceptance itself is a gift. This may be a helpful perspective, especially for men, as they seem to find it more difficult to give and receive love in a demonstrable way; in Western society, men have been acculturated not to show their feelings.

Love is a powerful force. Organizations would be healthier if their leaders could become more comfortable in both accepting and giving love. Men may wonder if the culture will ever reach a stage where they can do that and still be considered manly. We hope that will happen, but it may be difficult to achieve. Some women leaders, depending on their background, may shy away from accepting or showing love in a work environment for fear of being perceived as too feminine or too soft. We would argue that leaders need to be able to accept love and give it, regardless of their gender.

SHOWING YOU ARE GRATEFUL FOR THE OPPORTUNITY TO HELP OTHERS

One way to show you are grateful for the opportunity to help others is to do just that. If you have the opportunity to help, you've got to act, recognizing by definition that you are grateful for the chance. Be careful, however, to give your help with graciousness.

Paul has found that being helped by some people can be a painful process because they don't have that graciousness. It's as if they're saying, "Well, I'll help you, but it's a big inconvenience to me. I don't know quite why I'm even bothering, but I'll do it." Some helpers have such a sense of martyrdom and make such a big deal out of their assistance that you wish they hadn't bothered. When this happens, people are not grateful for the opportunity to help you; they see it as a burden rather than as a blessing. Gracious helpers would say, "I'm glad to be helping you, and it is something I truly want to do and not something I'm doing grudgingly."

We think that helping behavior is a natural inclination; children, for example, seem always to be glad for the opportunity to be helpful. There is something deep within people that wants to help others. Of course, not everybody needs help, and not everybody is open to accepting help, even when they need it, so you should be grateful for the opportunity to help someone. Judgment comes into play here. Like children who want to help but don't know what they're doing, grownups may also "help" in a way that doubles the work instead of cutting it in half. In such cases, you might find yourself telling the would-be helper, "I'd rather just do it myself." This is likely to hurt the helper. It means you are not valuing the giver's generosity, graciousness, and good intentions. Instead, you are looking only at the result of what they do.

A part of gratitude involves suspending judgment. Consider that if a child makes you something, you are grateful, even if it is a blotchy mess. You might also value the acts of kindness offered by other adults, regardless of the help's quality by focusing on the intention. American society puts a much larger premium on outcome than intention. Leaders should seek a balance between outcome and intention, so at least you appreciate both.

When you help someone, whether you help by offering a kind word, being a good listener when they need someone to talk to, lending your hand to physical tasks, or providing expertise, you feel good when that offer of help is accepted. When your help is rejected, you're left to wonder: Did they think I didn't have anything to offer, or did they think that the help came with strings and would obligate them? Why is it that my offer was not accepted? Did I misperceive that help was needed? It may be that the person you offered to help needed to be self-sufficient. If someone asks for your help, you might ask how you can be the most helpful to them. People often don't ask for help or accept its offer, so you may experience a natural feeling of gratefulness for the opportunity to share some aspect of yourself when your offer is accepted.

HOW YOU CAN SHOW YOU ARE GRATEFUL FOR YOUR GIFTS AND TALENTS

You can show you're grateful for your gifts and talents by using them. The notion of "use it or lose it" is also present in the biblical parable about coins, which interestingly were called *talents*. If the person buried talents, God was not pleased. You have to make use of what you have been given and try to expand and strengthen what you have. You do so through your actions as well as your words.

Gratitude for your gifts, in part, is about saying thank you. Genuine words of gratitude have power, but when you take your words a step further and align your "walk" and your "talk," their power increases. Being mindful of what your gifts are and accepting responsibility to develop them is a good way to show your gratitude. Gifts are rarely given in full-blown form. They must be cultivated and developed. Developing, using, and sharing your gifts constitutes both an opportunity and an obligation. You have an obligation to bring your gifts forward—not waste or hoard them—for your own benefit and the benefit of the world. The best way to show that you are grateful for your gifts is to share them.

Some people have a beautiful voice but won't sing in public; others are good cooks but won't prepare food for others. Too often, people have been given wonderful gifts but choose not to use them. Imagine if Paul said, "I have this gift of being able to speak to groups, small and large, but I choose not to speak anymore. I don't want to bother." Choosing not to use your gifts shows a lack of respect for the gift itself and for the giver. Whether you see your gifts as coming from your genetic heritage, from the Universe, from life, or from God, you have an obligation to develop and share them. The Bible admonishes, "To whom much is given, much is required." Those words remind you that your gifts are to be shared, not hoarded, and that the more you have been given, the more you have to share.

Everyone has gifts. People tend to define gifts narrowly; for example, "I'm really smart" or "I have a gift of being a great athlete or being able to sing or dance." Some of the most powerful people we know are some of the simplest people, but they've been given the gifts of love, generosity, and kindness, and they express those gifts. They may not be super smart or accomplished in other ways, but they are impressive. If you examine the critical people in any organization, people like these often come to mind.

Paul has such a person in his organization: Calvin, who runs the mailroom. If Calvin were not there, the organization would be markedly different, and not just because he does an efficient job of handling the mail. Paul might find another capable mailroom person, but he would have a hard time finding someone else with the generosity of spirit that Calvin brings to the organization. He constantly radiates a feeling of caring toward other people. Calvin shares that incredible gift every day with everyone in the organization. When people like Calvin die, large numbers

Suggestions for Action

- Make a list of some of your gifts and talents.
- Identify which of your gifts and talents are fairly well developed.
- Identify which of your gifts you would like to develop further.
- Identify which of your gifts you have largely shared with others.
- Identify which of your gifts you have yet to share with others in a significant way.
- Recall people in your life who helped you *identify* your gifts and talents, then express your gratitude.
- Recall people in your life who helped you *cultivate* your gifts and talents, then express your gratitude.
- Recall people in your life who helped you *share* your gifts and talents, then express your gratitude.
- If you are grateful to the Divine for your gifts and talents, express it in a way that is meaningful for you.

of people often attend their funerals. Their gift of their heart has an impact that is felt deeply and long remembered.

Paul received one of those little quizzes in the mail that makes you stop and think. It said: "Name the last five Pulitzer Prize winners, name the last five Heisman trophy winners, and name the last five Nobel Prize winners." Of course, most people can't do it. Then it said: "Name three teachers that made a difference in your life. Name five people who've loved you unconditionally and that made you feel special"—everyone can do that. And so then the question is: What's really important? Is it the accomplishment? Is it the talent expressed in the accomplishment of writing or running a football, or is it the talent expressed in making a difference in other people's lives, making their world richer, and making their sense of humanity more complete? Well, the answer is pretty clear, so talents are much broader than the way people often tend to view them.

ABOUT BEING GRATEFUL

At one level, gratefulness is a feeling, and from the feeling springs a desire to express that feeling. It can be expressed in words, images, or symbols, internally or externally—that you keep to yourself or that you share with other people or with the Universe. It can be expressed out loud or silently. You can demonstrate a level of appreciation or a feeling of gratefulness by presenting someone with a tangible gift. Our belief is that gratitude goes beyond these varied expressions of gratefulness, however; it is also an attitude—a mind-set. If you have an entitlement mentality rather than an attitude of gratitude, it is far less likely that you will experience feelings of gratefulness.

Gratitude emanates from the heart. When Paul has a feeling of gratitude, it starts somewhere in the middle of his chest, not in his head. When someone touches him through an act of kindness or does something that is meaningful to him, the meaning is made in his heart, not in his mind. Gratitude is one of the few things where the meaning is created at the emotional level much more than it is at the mental level. Gratitude is this welling up of a feeling in your heart, a sense of warmth and overflowing that occurs somewhere in your chest.

When that happens, gratitude is an expression of love—love writ large. If you take love in its largest context, when

Suggestions for Action

- Take a little time to think about what it means to be grateful.
- Take a little time to think about what you are grateful for.
- Take a little time to think about to whom you are grateful.
- Take a little time to think about why you are grateful.
- Take a little time to think about ways to express your gratitude.

someone behaves in a loving way toward you, in a way that shows they care, that they have a loving feeling toward you, or in a way that really helps you, their action tends to engender a feeling of gratitude. In this context, when you receive love and your heart is open to what you are receiving, it naturally evokes a feeling of gratitude. Let's consider, for a moment, the meaning of the word *gratitude*; people use some words so often that they don't take the time to think about their deeper meaning. Thinking about what it means to be grateful helps to open your heart to the feeling of gratefulness. So gratitude is related to love, and ultimately, every caring action is an expression of love in some profound way. When we use the word *love* here, we're looking at it from a broad perspective. Like countless others, we have come to have a very expansive view of the love in the world.

ENLIGHTENED LEADERS EXPERIENCE BOUNDLESS GRATITUDE

Boundless implies without boundaries. Enlightened leaders tend to be boundless in a lot of respects, and gratitude is just one of them. Enlightened leaders tend not to put boundaries around things but rather to remove the boundaries. What we are suggesting here is the kind of gratitude that can be endless and limitless, like an artesian well of possibility that just keeps pouring forth. If you put boundaries or limits on it, you're going to cap that well and limit what comes out, perhaps eventually shut it down entirely. If you do so, you will limit the potential for what might happen among the people in your organization. So starting with a sense of boundless gratitude is a way of letting that well spring forth, letting that water pour its healing powers over the land.

Gratitude is a well that never runs dry. When you give it away, you still have it—and just as much as you had when you started. Love is like that, too, and trust. Most, if not all, of the principles of enlightened leadership are like that. Because the ultimate source of

Suggestions for Action

- Think about leadership as a wellspring of *possibility*.
- Think about leadership as a wellspring of *hope*.
- Think about leadership as a wellspring of *optimism*.
- Think about leadership as a wellspring of *gratitude*.
- Remember that you never quite finish the "thank yous."
- Remember that gratitude is not an event, it is a process.
- Remember that you can never run out of gratitude.
- Remember that the more grateful you are, the more there will be to be grateful for.
- Remember that gratitude can be expressed through your thoughts, feelings, and actions.

enlightened leadership is divine wisdom, it would follow that the principles of enlightened leadership are boundless. In part, enlightened leadership is about touching those very things that enrich and broaden your existence and are not limiting or limited in any way. Boundless gratitude is just one.

What Might This Look Like in Practice?

How might leaders get in touch with their wellspring of boundless gratitude? One way is to realize how much you are the product of all the people and all the events that contributed to your experience. Who are the teachers who helped you become who you are? What did your parents do? What did your friends do? Who are the people in your life who have played a role in helping you become who you are and in developing your gifts and qualities? What we are suggesting is that if you have an attitude of, "Look, I've got all these gifts, I'm great, I did it all myself, I did it the hard way," you are not going to have much gratitude to give. But if you are aware that you received a lifetime of support, guidance, help, caring, love, and opportunity, then those ingredients contribute to the reciprocal notion of boundless gratitude. So many people have helped you in your lifetime, and some have passed on, so that the only way you can repay them is to pass their support along to others.

THE IMPORTANCE OF BEING GRATEFUL FOR DIVINE GUIDANCE

We believe that divine guidance is present regardless of your belief system. What varies is your awareness and acceptance of it, your sensitivity to it. But nonetheless, from our personal experience, we are convinced that divine guidance exists, operating in mysterious ways in everyone's lives. Clearly, some people do not subscribe to this view, and we respect that. However, there is an advantage to assuming that divine guidance does exist and to being grateful for it. In the same way that gratitude begets gratitude and strikes a responsive chord in others, a similar dynamic operates in relation to the Divine: The belief and acceptance of divine guidance, coupled with gratitude for that help, increases the divine guidance in your life. In other words, gratitude for divine guidance begets more divine guidance.

Being grateful for divine guidance implies that you believe in it and accept it. As a result, you tap into this incredible boundless source of possibility, a power source that would be frightening if it weren't so wonderful. You can't help but be grateful. If you truly have that sense of divine guidance at work in your life, your sense of optimism, inner peace, and acceptance will grow, too. You get this whole array of gifts with the one act of accepting divine guidance: You get the full package, a major "Blue Light Special."

We also believe that acceptance and gratitude for divine guidance determines how difficult or benign it will be, but the guidance is always there. If you choose not to accept it, divine guidance will still be there operating, but the lessons will be a whole lot tougher. Speaking figuratively, of course, it's banging your students on the head until you get their attention. We believe the Divine works the same way in presenting lessons and opportunities. If you accept them and are grateful, you move on to the next lesson. If not, you get into a "tough love" situation because you've got to get the lesson before you can move on to the next class. If you keep resisting, you'll have to stay after class longer, writing on the board a hundred times, "I will not ignore the lesson." On the other hand, having a sense of gratitude and embracing divine guidance allow you to move much more smoothly through to the next situation. The added bonus is that divine guidance gives you a sense of never being alone, of having the most powerful partner anyone could have, as well as an endless resource for wisdom.

SUMMARY

Gratitude is not only a powerful principle of leadership, it is an expression of love and connection between people and the world, and between human beings and the Divine. The well from which gratitude springs is limitless as are the opportunities for you to express it. The more grateful you are, the more grateful you become. The more gratitude you express, the more gratitude you receive. Genuine gratitude is empowering. It empowers you and those you lead. You are hard-wired with the capacity to both receive and express gratitude. As leaders, you can embody this principle and magnify its positive effects in the world.

The Principle of
Unique Life Lessons

Roseanne Roseannadanna, a character made famous by the late Gilda Radner on the popular *Saturday Night Live* show, used to observe, "It just goes to show. It's always something. If it's not one thing, it's something else." You are always experiencing something and, whether you like it or not, that "something" seems to be designed to promote your growth as a human being. Every time you learn one life lesson, life seems to conjure up a new one in an unrelenting cycle. There simply is no safe haven from the vicissitudes of life.

Nonetheless, you get to decide how you look at whatever comes your way—you can choose to see it as a problem or as an opportunity. Almost any problem can be seen as an opportunity to grow and learn. That doesn't mean the problem isn't difficult or painful or frustrating or aggravating or costly. It just means that there's a way to view or frame your experiences as opportunities for growth.

When we formed an organization called the Center for Enlightened Leadership, we checked with an attorney and were assured that no one had trademarked that name. We printed up letterhead, business cards, checks, invoices—all the material we would need to advance our principles of enlightened leadership—and filed a trademark application. As a consequence of that filing, a company named Enlightened Leadership International decided that we were infringing on their trademark. Our attorneys told us that we would most likely prevail if the matter were litigated but that it would cost us a lot of time and money. To borrow a line from an old cigarette commercial, our choice was to "fight or switch." After considerable discussion and consultation with friends and colleagues, we decided that fighting over the name wouldn't be very enlightened, and it was not where we wanted to put our energy. We chose to view what was happening as a test from the Universe—a life lesson to see if we could be more open and flexible, focusing on the larger mission. We changed our name to the Center for Empowered Leadership. To our surprise, almost everyone said they liked the new name even better. We opted to transmute the negative energy of a threatened lawsuit and to channel that energy into a more positive direction.

When either of us runs into difficulties, we ask ourselves, "Is there a lesson here? Is there some way I can learn and grow from this experience?" The potential lessons aren't always clear at first because they may be part of a larger pattern. But if they are important, they usually surface in a variety of places and circumstances. Paul had to get rid of a lot of things in his office and in his home for different reasons, but the pattern he saw was having too much clutter. If you are a packrat, as both of us are, it is hard to let go of things, but at times you have to do just that to make room for new things in your life. The larger concept here is to examine recurring problems for a discernable pattern that is calling you to change in some way.

In *Sacred Contracts*, best-selling author Caroline Myss says that people actually come to Earth with a contract that includes the lessons they want to learn, that people are all working on their own unique life lessons. This is Earth school, she asserts, and everyone has a curriculum designed to promote personal growth. Whether you agree with her perspective or not, it is a useful way of looking at the challenges and difficulties that confront you.

USING THE EXPERIENCES OF DAILY LIFE TO GROW PERSONALLY AND PROFESSIONALLY

In the context of life lessons, what happens in your personal and professional life gives you the opportunity to grow and to decide how you process those experiences in a way that actually promotes your growth. We are struck by the parallels in the lessons that we get personally and the lessons that we get professionally. They frequently are the same lessons at the same time. When you get into a certain space, it is as though the Universe brings it on no matter where you are, in the office or at home. There may be different renditions or tonalities, but it is all the same song. People tend to draw barriers between their professional and personal lives—what happens in one supposedly doesn't have anything to do with the other. We don't find that to be true.

The more reflective you are, the more you will have some awareness that a lesson is unfolding. You can learn to view the experiences in your personal and professional lives—both those you consider positive and those that seem problematic—as potential lessons for your own benefit and growth.

One of the difficulties many people have when they are confronted with a problem is that they start stepping forward to meet it when often more progress can be made by stepping back. If you train yourself to pause and step back as a challenge confronts you, you'll have a chance to look at the bigger picture and get a full appreciation of what you are up against. We know we are most effective when we stop and look at the whole situation first, even though human nature and all our training is telling us to get out our problem-solving tools and dig in. If you move too quickly, you might be busily solving something that isn't really the problem—or at least the right problem.

Sometimes solving the problem requires you to behave in a different way; in effect, to make a professional or personal change—a form of growth—in order to deal appropriately with whatever you encounter. Besides trying to use your skills to solve the problem, you can apply a lens that asks yourself whether something is happening that, in effect, might be a message from the Universe, something that is presenting you with an opportunity to grow. Unfortunately, people often externalize things, looking for solutions in the situation instead of asking themselves, "Is there something internal, within me, that needs to change?"

People tend to resist life's lessons instead of embracing them. Paul knows that he is most effective when he embraces a problem. Sometimes he will say, "What a great problem, bring it on. Bring it on and let me fully appreciate the whole thing." When you do that, problems sometimes seem to shrink and shrivel up, even disappear, even though they seemed so huge. Embracing a lesson allows you to get it and move on, whereas if you resist it, you can't get past it. The problem becomes a wall standing in your way; when you bring the problem toward you, you'll soon find yourself standing on the other side.

When you embrace a problem, it is important to recognize that there may be a lesson operating as well. You are the participant, but you are also the observer in your own life. As you step back in the role of observer to gain perspective, think about what lessons may be unfolding for you.

Well-known author Wayne Dyer likens problems to a little blue-haired lady driving in front of you, slowing you down. The tendency is to get aggravated with her because you're not getting where you need to get. According to Dyer, the best response is to say, "She's here to teach me something. What's the lesson? Maybe I should have left earlier. Maybe I've got to plan ahead better." The obstacles that come into your life often have lessons to teach, and it is up to you, first of all, to figure out just what the right lesson is.

This was driven home to Paul when he was struggling with a difficult board member. One of the lessons Paul was hearing was that he needed to oversee his staff more diligently and get them to be more detail-oriented. Doing so might decrease the pain and pressure he was feeling, but Paul didn't think that was the right lesson, and he resisted that direction. Imposing tighter oversight is a disempowering approach and runs counter to his belief system and philosophy. In this case, the real lesson was staying true to his beliefs in the face of enormous pressure. Grabbing the right lesson from a situation can be difficult. You have to study the problem thoroughly so you don't attack an apparent lesson instead of the real one underneath it.

PEOPLE ARE GIVEN LIFE LESSONS TO PROMOTE SPIRITUAL GROWTH

We firmly believe that this Earth school and everything in it offers life lessons to promote our spiritual growth. Every obstacle, every stumbling block, is in essence a steppingstone for greater growth. Sometimes it is really easy to lose sight of that and to get put off by something because it hurts or it is hard. Earth school is different from regular school. In school, you get the lesson first and then you get the test, whereas in life, you get the test first, and then you get the lesson. Earth school is a tougher environment because you are always being tested so you can learn and grow, and the only way you can do that is through challenge. Think of it as spiritual isometrics. You've got to keep pushing and pulling to build the spiritual muscle you need to move forward.

The same lens we suggested for personal and professional growth can also be applied to spiritual growth. When life is difficult or things don't feel right, you can ask yourself, "What is the spiritual lesson that I need to pay attention to?" It may be helpful to ask that question out loud, addressing it to the Universe at large, because as we said earlier, the lesson is not always readily apparent. Sometimes it takes deep reflection or even prayer to gain insight as to just what the lesson is— whether you need to open up or loosen up or find a better balance, to be more compassionate, or whatever. The variety of lessons created to assist in your spiritual growth is virtually limitless. One of your challenges is to identify and understand the nature of the lesson at hand; when you do, you've taken an important step toward learning what you need to know. You could think of life as learning a series of skills. Then ask yourself, "What skill do I need to cultivate to meet the particular challenges that I am being confronted with at this moment in my life?" This is a lens or perspective that everyone can apply to the events of life.

What Might This Look Like in Practice?

When Paul was diagnosed with glaucoma, it did two things for him. First, it gave him a great metaphor for leadership because glaucoma is all about the pressure building up in your eye so that you start to lose your vision gradually over time. Paul saw this happening to leaders as they face pressure: They lose their vision so gradually they don't know it is being lost. Glaucoma gave him a great metaphor for explaining that to people. The second gift was that having glaucoma helped him to see things more clearly. When you are worried about whether or not you will continue to see, you suddenly pay a lot more attention to what you are looking at; it becomes much more precious. Paul began to see things more clearly and more intensely, stepping back to appreciate and enjoy what he could see. He didn't take his sight for granted. So the challenge of the glaucoma was actually a wonderful gift.

A lot of life lessons operate in the same way. They allow you to stop, pay attention, and see things more clearly than you did before you confronted those challenges. This happens to many people who face sickness. When the wife of Paul's friend in Tucson was diagnosed with cancer, the friend was forced to choose what was most important to him—his job or his wife; a difficult decision. Paul's friend found it a clarifying experience, being confronted with the choices he needed to make instead of just lollygagging through life trying to be all things to all people simultaneously. Many of life's lessons do that for you.

When Steve's children were young, his children were relating to each other and to their mother in a disruptive way. It turned out that Steve needed to create a better balance between his work life and home life. He was giving too much time and energy to his professional life and not enough to the needs of his family. Fortunately, with the help of his brother Adam, who is a psychotherapist, he was able to clarify the life lesson and to create a better balance, which required change and growth on his part. A shift became possible as a result of asking the question, "What is the root cause of the problem in our family?" Once the underlying cause became clear, Steve's willingness to make different choices brought about a healthier family life.

> ## Suggestions for Action
>
> - Identify an experience in your *professional* life that had the effect of promoting your spiritual growth.
> - Identify an experience in your *personal* life that had the effect of promoting your spiritual growth.
> - Recall a time when overcoming a difficulty helped you become a better human being.
> - Recall a time when overcoming a great difficulty helped you feel more connected to life.
> - Identify an experience that helped you become a better person.
> - Identify an experience that helped you evolve in a positive way.
> - Look for a metaphor or story line that gives greater meaning to your life's experiences.
> - As you have significant life experiences, ask yourself, "What is the lesson here?"
> - Increase the time you spend in active reflection about your life's experiences.

PROBLEMS ARE ACTUALLY OPPORTUNITIES IN DISGUISE

Problems can be seen as lessons that can move you forward, sometimes even creating breakthroughs that promote dramatic growth. We subscribe to the notion that no door closes without another opening. There are patterns and cycles to life. What looks like a great negative often turns out to be a great positive because it opens up the next step in your life. It is the door to the next opportunity. Paul's personal life offers a good case in point. The ending of one relationship opened up the possibility of another much better one. So what could have been seen as a sad negative experience because of one relationship ending actually was a wonderful prelude to the next possibility. One of the key issues here is how you view life.

We are inveterate pony finders. People like us are always looking to find the pony and overlooking the horse manure while others just focus on the horse manure. Can you turn people who focus on manure into pony finders? We hope so. We are the eternal optimists, ever hopeful that many of the things we've learned others can learn also.

We worry about any leader who isn't the most optimistic person in the organization. Any leader who doesn't see hope and possibility as opposed to fear and problems is really the biggest problem of all. Yet some leaders can't do that. They are in leadership positions, but they may not be leaders. Leaders have to cultivate optimism, which is why this principle—seeing problems as opportunities—is so important. It is the possibility behind the problem that offers hope. Any organization led by a pessimist or a cynic is usually headed in the wrong direction.

One of the attributes of enlightened leadership is an awareness that all problems have opportunities and possibilities embedded within them. Just as an embedded order lies within chaos, a principle of chaos theory, a kernel of something positive lies within negative events. To activate it, you have only to look for it, identify it as such, and then empower it by giving it energy. The enlightened leader is charged with showing people that positive potential.

We all lived through the events of 9/11. Certainly this was one of the most terrible things that has ever happened on American soil and yet, within that, has been the opportunity for bravery, heroism, people coming together, outpourings of generosity, caring, and compassion, a renewed sense of patriotism, and the resolve to defeat international terrorism. If this most horrific event has positive potentialities, then the same can be true of any problem.

Like the Chinese symbol for yin and yang—a small black dot in a field of white, and a small white dot in a field of black—every weakness has an inherent strength built into it. Every human flaw is linked to a strength. If you want to know a person's greatest strength, look behind his or her flaw. Of course, the opposite is also true. Look behind everyone's greatest strength, and you'll also see the greatest weakness. Because those two things are inextricably tied together, you can always take one and turn it into the other. Tony Robbins, an authority on peak performance, does that when he talks about limiting beliefs. He says that everyone has limiting beliefs but that these can be turned into empowering beliefs.

Robbins talks about his own limiting beliefs when he was first starting out in business. For example, his perceptions that he was young and uneducated were two limiting beliefs. So he told himself, "Well, I'm young, that means I've got lots and lots of time, more than most people. I have lots of time to do what I want to get done, and I'm not educated, which means that I'm not limited by teachings that may have limited my ability to see things more clearly. Because of a lack of education, I'm able to look at things with fresh eyes." He took the negatives and turned them into positives.

What Might This Look Like in Practice?

When Steve was 24 years old, he was given the opportunity to serve as the director of a residential school-camp for brain-damaged and emotionally disturbed children. He hired a lot of young people as teachers and coun-

selors, people with high energy and creative ideas about fun-filled, life-enhancing things they would like to do with children who had special needs. Together, they put together a program in which these special-needs children would sleep in cabins, eat in a mess hall, go on overnight camping trips, put up tents, chop wood— the full range of activities that you would find in any typical residential camp setting. They assumed that these children could do anything that children without special needs could do, if they created the right conditions and structured the activities with care. Before long, trained psychologists were coming to see what Steve's team was doing that enabled the

> ### Suggestions for Action
>
> - Identify a problem and then ask yourself what opportunities open as a result of this problem.
> - In a group setting, ask your staff not to focus on solving a given problem but instead to focus on the opportunities embedded in the problem for good things to emerge.
> - Conduct scenarios with your staff to help them learn how to see positive potentialities within negative events.

children to eat family-style, take responsibility for cleaning their bunks, and enjoy activities that others thought they would not be able to do. It was all in the team's belief system: They looked at each problem as an opportunity for the staff to solve with love, compassion, and creativity. They did not let limiting beliefs determine the experiences and activities that they would provide for the children they were serving. Consequently, the children and the staff grew in remarkable ways.

We see limiting beliefs in schools all the time, with schools limiting kids' possibilities based on assumptions about what they can do and based on external variables, but not based on the reality of the internal possibilities of people.

CLOUDS DO HAVE SILVER LININGS

Of course, some people believe that behind every silver lining there is a dark cloud, but we have seen the silver linings in clouds. Consider Nature: Clouds bring rain, and rain makes it possible for things to grow. Besides the metaphor of rain producing life, you have the rainbow, a metaphorical symbol of possibility and promise that often follows the storm. You can't have rainbows, however, unless you have rain, so you've got to have clouds. All negative things tend to have embedded within them a positive thing and the possibility of a sunnier day. Remember the metaphor of the valleys and the mountains: The valleys help give meaning to the mountain heights. You've got to have contrast, and that is a hard lesson for human beings to understand. Contrast generates meaning, and you can only have contrasts by having negatives. If you just had silver linings, they would be meaningless. The tension of the contrasts in life creates the possibility for the silver linings to emerge.

As we have said, it is important for leaders to view problems as opportunities in disguise. So the question becomes, "When things are cloudy, what is the silver lining?" If you don't ask yourself that question, you may miss it. How do you take advantage of the cloud? Enlightened leaders are able to take advantage of the darkness. Accomplishing this takes more than just seeing that light can come from something dark; it also requires the proactive ability to create a better day. You can do that by not allowing the clouds to deter you, by seizing the negative moment and turning it around.

What Might This Look Like in Practice?

Let's return to the camp for special needs children where Steve was the director. He and his staff decided to create a petting zoo for the children. He told the children that it would open on a certain date; predictably, they were excited. Steve had arranged for little lambs and goats, a baby calf, and other little critters to be delivered on that date, and of course, he needed pens for the animals. As luck would have it, stormy weather arrived several days before the baby animals were scheduled for delivery. Steve organized his staff and said, "Let's put on our raingear and get to work." They all went out in the pouring rain to build the pens needed for the zoo. One of his staff members said someday Steve should write a book called *Building Goat Pens in the Rain* because he had made a promise, and he was not going to allow the stormy weather to interfere. His team worked through torrents of water. Everything was muddy, dark, cold, and wet, but the camp counselors refused to be deterred because they could foresee the silver lining: the joy on the children's faces when the rain stopped and the sun came out and the children had their very own petting zoo. Here was a case where Steve and his staff literally did not allow the clouds to deter them, and together, they found the silver lining at the end of the rainbow.

If leaders not only ask themselves to look for the silver lining in cloudy times but also encourage the people they work with to do so, there will be a multiplier effect. As groups of people begin to think about negative events and circumstances, they may see different silver linings in the same cloud. It becomes a challenge to ask people, "What are the positive opportunities here, or what is the silver lining, and can we find it?" Answering that question becomes a growth opportunity, and it also produces silver linings.

> **Suggestion for Action**
>
> - Create a training exercise where people are confronted with negative situations, and ask them to create positive situations out of the negative to help them become possibility thinkers.

LEARNING LIFE'S LESSONS THE HARD WAY OR THE EASY WAY

When you are given a choice of learning life's lessons, your own reaction sets the stage for what unfolds. You can resist the lesson, which makes it a lot harder: Resistance creates friction, friction creates heat, and heat burns. Or you can embrace it, which makes it easier. When you resist a lesson, you end up burning yourself, whereas when you embrace it and bring it toward you, it may not be an easy lesson, but it may not take you as long to get it. You can move past it and on to the next place. Your attitude about lessons determines how hard or how easy they are. Some people have extremely hard lives but are able to work through it, whereas others haven't had that much difficulty, but every problem is magnified. It is not the lessons themselves as much as the reaction to the lessons that makes it difficult; some people do make mountains out of molehills, whereas other people make molehills out of mountains. A lot of it has to do with your resilience and maybe even the depth of your faith. People with a strong sense of faith often find that the lessons are easier, less overwhelming, and of shorter duration.

Many people aren't aware that they are confronting a life lesson, or they may even deny what is happening. In denial, you don't even see what is being presented, or you ignore it or simply rationalize it away. But the Universe is mysteriously constructed in such a way that if this is one of your lessons, it will not go away just because you ignore it. In a sense, the lesson relentlessly pursues you, and it may change form or escalate until it reaches a point where you cannot ignore it. A physical illness may be treated fairly easily if you go to the doctor and take the prescribed remedy, but if you ignore the symptoms and warning signs, it becomes more serious over time and then something that was minor becomes acute or even chronic.

Paul used to get a kick out of the people in Tucson who had moved to the Sunbelt for a new beginning, to get away from their problems. They would get there and, of course, their problems were still with them because they were the source of their problems. Sometimes, these people would be bitter because they had moved across the country to start fresh and found they had the same problems they hoped to leave back home. Paul kept wanting to say, "Hey, there is no reason to be upset. You brought the problems with you, dude; they're your problems. They aren't somebody else's." The real question is how do you start fresh? If you want to get rid of your problems, you've got to get rid of a part of yourself that is no longer serving you. You've got to start with yourself, and if you don't do that, your problems just intensify and get bigger.

Suggestions for Action

- Remember that the more you resist a life lesson, the more it will repeat itself and intensify.
- When you encounter significant problems in your health, job, relationships, and so forth, look for a pattern to discern a possible life lesson.
- When you find yourself being defensive, look for a pattern to see if a life lesson keeps popping up.
- Remember that once a lesson is identified, resolving it invariably requires some change in your behavior.
- Remember to be patient with yourself because mastering a life lesson may not be easy.
- Remember that self-awareness and openness are two keys to mastering life lessons.
- In times of difficulty, try to step back and detach from your ego to gain a clearer vision of what is unfolding.
- In times of difficulty, look to people you trust to give you honest feedback and to hold up an accurate mirror of what is unfolding.

What Might This Look Like in Practice?

Ego plays an important role in how people respond to problems connected to their life lessons. In our experience, the more your ego gets engaged in the process, the more likely you are to miss the lesson. Paul recalls a former colleague who was extremely talented, bright, creative, and hard working but had a tremendous ego along with a need to be in control. This individual would drive people away and create conflict as a result of those two issues. Paul had a number of discussions with her about how self-destructive those behaviors were and how they undermined her own talents. The individual responded, "That's just the way I am. I'm not going to change."

Ultimately, Paul had to ask the person to leave the organization because her destructive nature was interfering with everyone else's ability to get work done. In Paul's view, this was tragic because that person's ego needs got in the way of her understanding that she needed to modify some of her behaviors to grow and become more effective. In this case, refusing to learn a life lesson made matters worse and, ultimately, cost her a job.

Leaders need to consider the problems that are occurring in their lives or in their organizations and ask, "How can I address these things at the lowest possible level before they grow, and grow in the wrong ways?" The next question is, "How am I creating this or contributing to this?" Their own role is the last thing most people look at because, by and large, people tend to look outside of themselves for the causes of difficulties they face.

Paul has a friend who is always accusing him of being dispassionate, and Paul acknowledges that there is certainly a lot of that in him. But dispassion can be appropriate because you need dispassion to ask yourself, "What am I doing to create this?" If you are not somewhat dispassionate about raising that question, you tend to get your ego involved. The question takes the form of, "What's wrong with me?" There's a difference between that question and "What am I doing to create the problem?" People always create problems for themselves, but there's nothing wrong with them. What's wrong—and right— with them is that they're human like everyone else. To counter the tendency to blame yourself, dispassion lets you step back and say, "I'm not going to blame myself for this; I'm just going to assess it and try to change it."

Paul often looks at a problem and says objectively what he needs to do to change the situation without taking a lot of personal blame for it. This drives some people crazy because they want him to just get down and grovel for being wrong, as opposed to saying, "Well, that's not working right, let's change it." Again, the key is to acknowledge that something isn't working the way you want it to, then make a shift without a lot of self-blame and recrimination.

USING THE WEAKNESSES WITHIN STRENGTHS TO UNDERSTAND LIFE LESSONS

Knowing that the weaknesses within your strengths can help you to understand your life lessons points you in a direction where you are the least likely to look. As you think about yourself and the people in your organization, you identify your perceived strengths. This is something people are comfortable doing because they're at ease discussing what they are good at. People tend not to realize that blind spots are embedded within those strengths, and these can cause problems. By definition, you can't see what's in your blind spot—for example, think of your rear-view mirror and how cars can be so close and yet you don't see them in the mirror. You have to turn your head and look. It's just as important to keep an extra watchful eye on your personal strengths because something lurking there might trip you up if you're not careful. When it does—and it usually does at some point—you have a good opportunity to look for a lesson there.

Whatever you do best hides an inherent weakness. For example, a person who is humanistic will sometimes hesitate to make a tough decision or do something that will be hurtful to someone but still needs to be done. So that extreme humanism can make you overly sensitive. There is a teaching in Taoism that too much emphasis on being pretty makes you ugly—too much emphasis on anything that is positive shows up as a weakness in that same thing. For example, someone who is good at making money could end up by being greedy, and so on.

What Might This Look Like in Practice?

Paul tends to be humane and a nurturing "grow them" kind of leader. He wants to see people emerge and grow—a great strength. Over the years, he has been able to develop a lot of people and help them emerge into their possibilities. But sometimes he has allowed bad situations to go too far in the hopes that things will turn around. Remember the example of the employee who let her own ego get in the way of her performance. Paul later concluded that he should have removed that person from the organization several years before he did, and he thinks that the organization was harmed by his hope that somehow this person would change her ways when everyone but Paul could see that was just not going to happen. He failed to recognize that this was an instance where a strength actually created a weakness and made a tough situation even harder to resolve.

One of Steve's strengths is that he can look at a complex problem or issue and frequently see a solution or some path through it almost instantaneously. He has found that if he gives people the answer, they don't have a clue as to how he got there. He's like the math student who knows the answer but has difficulty explaining his reasoning. So his strength in terms of processing problems or options quickly has an embedded weakness in that the people around him may misunderstand or misconstrue what is actually happening. They may think Steve isn't taking the time to think things through or to consider options suggested by others; they may believe his solution is unworkable. One of Steve's lessons has been to take the time to articulate a process that is self-evident to him so that others will understand not only where he wants to go but also how he arrived at his solutions. Steve thought it was a waste of his time to explain himself until he realized that people had no way of knowing what was going on inside his mind and what options he was considering unless he revealed and articulated his thought processes by taking his internal dialogue and sharing it in an external way.

When people appreciate what they are good at, they tend to overlook that problems may arise in this blind spot. They say, "I'm really good at such and such; it's one of my strengths, so let's focus on something else." You may be inclined to assume that you don't have to focus on areas where you are strong. It seems counterintuitive that you could be weak or vulnerable in areas where you are strong, and it may be the last place you look for the source of a problem even though it may be the most fruitful. As we said earlier, this is a fractal that mirrors the relationship between chaos and order. In James Gleick's book *Chaos*, he explains that although the universe reflects the most wonderful order at different levels of magnitude, the seeds of chaos are also embedded there. Conversely, the seeds of naturally emerging order are embedded in chaos. As the universe features an ongoing dance between chaos and order, so people's lives display an ongoing dance between their weaknesses and strengths.

MASTERY OF EACH LIFE LESSON OPENS A GATEWAY TO THE NEXT

Opportunities for personal growth continue throughout life as one lesson leads to another. In other words, life's lessons are never finished. The corollary to old-timer baseball catcher Yogi Berra's observation, "It's not over until it's over," is that it is never over because each thing leads to the next. Ironically, the mastery of a life lesson—or its failure—leads to the next thing. The difference is that with mastery, you move on to a new lesson whereas failure means you repeat the lesson, and it intensifies. As in school, if you fail the lesson, you have to go back a grade instead of being promoted, and you get a tougher teacher as well. Mastery, on the other hand, means promotion to the next grade and maybe even graduation to the next level of schooling, but in the school of life, you never graduate in the sense that you are finished. Rather than graduation, you have a commencement, a new beginning.

Life is structured so that the ceiling of one level of mastery becomes the floor of the next, like going from the top class in junior high school to

Suggestions for Action

- Be mindful that as you master each lesson, you have a more sophisticated tool kit at your disposal.
- Be mindful that as you grow as a human being, you grow in your ability to master subtlety and nuance in life's lessons.
- Be mindful that as you grow as a human being, your life's lessons increase in depth and complexity.
- Be mindful that as you grow as a human being, the domains and context (such as health, work, family, relationships, finances, etc.) of your life lessons increase.
- Be mindful that living life from a spiritual orientation requires you to embrace your life lessons rather than pull away from them.

the bottom class in high school. Throughout your life, this happens over and over. Embedded in this whole dynamic process is the notion of movement: If you don't continue to grow, then you stagnate. Lack of movement creates stagnation, an inherently unhealthy state. Stagnant water breeds disease. Things that are not moving are dying. So it is important not only to go from lesson to lesson, but also to stay in motion by being actively engaged in working through life's lessons. You will never reach a stage where you have no new lessons to confront—no matter how wealthy or healthy or successful you are.

ENDINGS CREATE THE OPPORTUNITY FOR NEW BEGINNINGS

When Steve's friend got divorced after being married for 20 years, he went through a grieving process over the loss of the relationship. In the end, however, the divorce gave him the opportunity to relocate in another part of the country where he could devote his attention to his mother and sister, who were both debilitated due to serious illness. As events in your life come to the end of some cycle, you often find an opening for other events to unfold. Not only in divorce but with other endings—the loss of a job or even the loss of a loved one—the ending is always tied to a new beginning. What you do with those new opportunities is always up to you. The adage "When one door closes, another one opens" sums up a helpful perspective. You may be so focused on the ending or the loss you are experiencing that you may fail to recognize the doorway of opportunity that is opening. There is also a saying that you should not let the door hit you in the butt on your way out. Well, you should take care not to let it hit you in the butt while it is opening to possibilities. Focusing on the closing door is limiting and dangerous.

The whole cycle of life is rooted in beginnings and endings. Endings give rise to new beginnings and, conversely, you can't have a beginning without the eventual prospect of an ending. Enlightened leaders help people look at endings with an eye toward recognizing the opportunities for new beginnings. They also help people understand that even as things begin, the natural cycle will lead to closure; this is part and parcel of the natural cycle of endings and beginnings in the universe, with each creating the opportunity for the other.

This perspective is also useful in thinking about change and change-oriented leaders. Change-oriented leaders understand the natural relationship between endings and new beginnings, and they lead from that premise. Other leaders don't see change as natural and are more status-quo oriented. They try to hold on to a particular end and block natural endings. And, of course, the irony is that you can't because the harder you try to hold on to something, the more it runs through your fingers.

SUMMARY

You may have heard the line "Be patient with me, I'm a work in progress." Or, "Be patient with me, God's not finished with me yet." These both suggest that as human beings you are continually growing and changing, hopefully for the better. This raises the question: Is there a process designed to promote your growth as a human being? We think there is. We think life is a series of ongoing experiences designed to do just that. Your role is to recognize this process and to live your life, both professionally and personally, in a reflective manner that allows you to discern the lessons and make whatever changes you need to make to grow and evolve into better and better versions of yourself. You get the lessons, and you get the ability to discover the opportunities for growth, and you are given all the tools you need to process them, but ultimately, the choices about what you do as a result of your lessons is your own. You, and those whose lives you touch, reap the consequences of the choices you make.

The Principle of a Holistic Perspective

Perhaps you've heard the story about the three blind men who came across an elephant in the forest. As the story goes, one reached out and caught the tail, one grabbed hold of a leg, and the other grabbed hold of the elephant's trunk. The first man thought he was touching a vine, the second a tree trunk, and the third a large snake. The problem, of course, was that each had a limited perspective, and none could see how the parts were related to the whole.

Leaders are inevitably dealing with people who perceive only one part of the elephant. Your job is not only to see the whole and how the parts contribute to it but also to help others see it. Think of this in terms of connections and context. From the leader's vantage point, you are in a position not only to see the connections but also to create them. Your job is to create the structures that bring people together for collaboration and to open the communication pathways in all directions. By bringing diverse elements of your organization together for dialogue[1] and by setting a tone of mutual respect, you can help people gain a more holistic perspective on the issues that confront them. In your leadership role, you get to set the context or framework for whatever is unfolding. You always want to do that from the highest perspective, a perspective that asks people to look at the whole, to look at the parts, and to look at the relationship of the parts to each other and to the whole.

As you know, people want to be meaningfully involved in decisions that affect their lives. You need to create processes that let the people who see the tail talk with both the people who see the trunk and the people who see the legs. When you also help them to ask questions from a holistic perspective regarding the way these elements affect each other and relate to the whole, staff members are more likely to realize they are working with an elephant—a truly powerful creature that can't be taken lightly and one whose long-term memory is legendary. To put it another way, when people begin to see holistically, they tend to be more understanding of diverse perspectives. And when people are involved in meaningful ways in collaborative processes, this helps create positive long-term institutional memory of both the process and the outcomes.

What Might This Look Like in Practice?

Leaders work with systems in which the components are connected and affect one another. People tend to see things from their own perspective. It's your job to help people see things from a larger, more holistic perspective.

In the mid 1990s, Steve's school system decided to take a year to explore the issue of block scheduling at the high school level, using a holistic perspective. Interdisciplinary committees were formed to look at different scheduling patterns and the implications for the curriculum, staff development, budget, and contractual obligations. Minutes from all the committee meeting were kept and shared. The staff was invited to pose questions to any of the committees. Answers were generated, and ample time was created for discussion and information sharing among committee members. Each committee prepared an oral and written report of its findings and recommendations, which were shared with the entire faculty and later with the school board. Block scheduling was successfully implemented in the district's high school, partly due to the holistic process that was used. From a holistic perspective, the change process itself often affects the outcome, and in many respects, how change is accomplished can be as important as the actual outcome in the minds of those involved.

SPIRITUAL TRUTHS IN THE STORY OF THREE BLIND MEN AND THE ELEPHANT

Where you stand on an issue depends on where you sit. People fix on particular positions and become adamant to the point where arguments, disagreements, and even wars are generated by differences of perspective. People have their own version of the truth. One of the spiritual truths about the metaphor of the blind men is that they are blind. Isn't everyone? People all think they know the truth, when in fact they are all operating from a limited perspective that makes them blind in many ways. Their childhood environment, their life experiences, their prejudices, their need to be right, and to some extent their sense of superiority—all of these lead to a form of blindness.

In the story, each man grabs a different part of reality, and that becomes the basis of how he looks at things when what the men really needed was a broader perspective. Had they shared their information more effectively, they might have been able to piece together the creature they were encountering instead of all arguing about the relative truth as each perceived it. If only they hadn't jumped to a conclusion based on a limited perspective, they might have resolved their seemingly different realities through collaboration. If they had viewed the situation as a puzzle, allowing for the possibility that they all might hold a different part of the solution, and if they had questioned each other, looking more deeply with their other senses, they might have come to the realization they were experiencing something that was made up of multiple parts as opposed to saying, "No, it's long and skinny, or round and thick, or curved and hairy."

The metaphor shows that people can perceive different truths based on the limited information that they have. From their respective vantage points, all of the men thought they were right, but they were all wrong. Yes, they gave a plausible explanation of what they were experiencing, but their vision wasn't large enough—and it could have been expanded by collaboration and sharing.

In this case, all of the pieces of the truth are connected—in fact, inseparable—but the blind men don't know it. By segmenting the elephant, they can't discern its true nature. Most people look at reality in the same way, failing to understand that it is part of a holistic interconnectedness. If you take the pieces apart, you don't have that reality anymore. You have something less than the reality, and in fact, you kill the reality when you chop it up through a reductionist perspective.

The parable of the three blind men and the elephant shows what happens when people have a limited perspective. Contrast the men with leaders who have a holistic perspective. When you look at things holistically, you examine them from all sides and all vantage points, looking at the positive and negative truths from that inclusive perspective.

Appreciative Leaders (edited by Bea Mah Holland, et al.) has a subtitle that says: "In the Eye of the Beholder." We are convinced that many of the problems in education stem from the fact that some beholders have such a limited perspective. This is especially true with respect to the issue of governance, which from a holistic perspective affects everything else. As a leader, you must strive to help people see things from more than one perspective, which requires more openness and more collaboration. You might benefit from the wisdom expressed by Atticus Finch, played by Gregory Peck in the movie *To Kill a Mockingbird*: "You never really know a man until you stand in his shoes and walk around in them." Once you can see things as though you are standing in other people's shoes, you can help others do it, too.

Although putting yourself in the shoes of another may be useful, we have found that one of the best strategies is to ask people "What does this looks like through your eyes?" We are frequently surprised by what they say. When they tell us what it looks like through their eyes, we may not agree with their perspective, but it is one of the best ways we know of getting a true sense of what their perspective is. Understanding the other person's point of view may or may not help you to find common ground, but at the very least, communication will be enhanced and people will have a sense that they have been heard.

What Might This Look Like in Practice?

As a leader, Paul tries to keep lightness in the dialogue: He uses humor as his secret weapon. When working with teams—whether the team was his cabinet as a superintendent or the senior members of the organization he leads—he creates a certain lightness in the culture of the team itself for two reasons. One, it is more fun, and two, a little humor can help the very different personalities on your team work together. Part of the power of a good team comes from having different talents, skill sets, and approaches available. A light-hearted tone and the use of humor make it easier for different voices to hear one another.

As long as the three blind men are strongly asserting their opinions and giving each other very little credence, you have almost no possibility of achieving a true description of the elephant. That becomes possible only when the three blind men are willing to listen to each other and say, "Wait a minute, let's put these pieces together." You might inject some lightness into your team meeting by telling the story and then asking them to consider what the heck the elephant was thinking while all this was going on. Here are three guys pulling on different parts of his anatomy, all convinced that they've got the answer to what he is all about, and none of them, to paraphrase Atticus Finch, has ever stood in his hooves. In addition, there is the perspective of the observer who is watching both the elephant and the three blind men. The inner vision from the elephant's perspective and the outer vision from someone who can see it all, when taken together, yield a truly holistic perspective.

Keeping lightness in the elephant story is to remember that if you go around pulling an elephant's tail or trunk, the elephant will eventually get annoyed and step on you! Wholeness in thinking is a safer way to go, but you can only do that if people feel they can be open about their perspectives without getting chopped up in the process. Paul uses a lot of humor in meetings because it helps people feel

Suggestions for Action

- When you are dealing with tough decisions, try to get as many diverse viewpoints as you can to help you see things from different perspectives.
- Listen and be open to the truths of others.
- Look for the connections between diverse perspectives.
- Create open two-way communication systems that are inviting rather than off-putting with easy access for people.
- Make sure that the two-way flow of information throughout your organization is timely.
- Use phrases such as: "Can you tell me more about what you see?" or, "Tell me more about that."

relatively safe. If things get a little too uptight or the dialogue is growing inflated and out of control, poking a needle into it lets some of the air out.

ENLIGHTENED LEADERS ARE AWARE THAT EVERYTHING IS CONNECTED

Good leaders have a capacity to know things that they sometimes find hard to describe. It is what Malcolm Gladwell, in his book *Blink,* calls tacit knowledge. These leaders see the strategic connections among seemingly unrelated circumstances and are able to operate with an understanding of those connections. Good leaders can make a decision on one track knowing that it affects four other tracks at the same time. And they know that when they are making a decision over in right field, left field is being affected as well. The best leaders have a holistic view; they think strategically but *strategic* in a different sense of the word. They can see the potential ripples flowing from their actions and can anticipate not only where the connections are but also where the impact can and will be felt because they have the opposite of tunnel vision. They have a 360-degree, multifiltered lens that allows them to see the inherent structure and connections in most situations.

Such leaders are often called visionaries. In addition to having a perspective that sees foreground and background, they see the connections both as they are and as they can be, so they actually see a double lattice. They see not only where things are already interconnected but also where a few more open lines could create something even better. It is like seeing a not fully completed wiring diagram. There is a pole here and a pole there, but the path between them isn't hooked up yet.

What Might This Look Like in Practice?

Paul used to have a lot of trouble with his staff because he would start with several different initiatives that, in his mind, were woven together. However, in the real world, most people couldn't see the connection between them. In fact, it would take two to three years for those interconnections to become obvious to everybody else. For example, he might see the way a specific reading program and a training program and certain initiative with the community might play off of each other, long before those connections were actually realized.

Some people need to experience things firsthand; they can't see where the connections might be because they are still isolated in their thinking. One of the problems with being a visionary is helping people to grasp your vision, as least in the early stages. People don't see what you see, they don't know what you know, and you may find it difficult to convey your vision. This situation is captured in a wonderful line from the movie *Butch Cassidy and the Sundance Kid,* where Butch Cassidy says, "I've got vision, and the rest of the world is wearing bifocals."

If you aren't aware that everything is connected, you may be one of those people who are wearing metaphorical bifocals. Without that awareness, your perspective is limited, and your potential for serious error is magnified. If you are leading an organization and you don't understand that things are connected, it is a recipe for disaster. One of our mottos is: Unrelated actions have related consequences. In a school system, you may think you are revising the sex education curriculum, but you may also be electing the next school board because these things are often interconnected. Invariably, some people will be honing in on the elephant's leg instead of drawing back to see the whole elephant.

Paul recalls a meeting where some of his staff members were insisting that the organization deal with an issue that very day. He knew that doing so would have been a total disaster because the issue was going to be controversial, the groundwork had not been done, and the timing was not right. First, the proximity of the issue to a scheduled discussion concerning Paul's contract could spill over with unrelated and unintended consequences. Second, Paul was getting ready to start a four-day conference and didn't want to begin with a topic that would create acrimony within the executive committee. Paul told his staff the item under consideration could wait a few days or even a few weeks. But his staff kept insisting on the perceived righteousness of their position without seeing how it related to other events and relationships.

This happens a lot in organizations where people don't understand that one action is tied to another and that seemingly unrelated things like the leg and the tail are actually connected to the same elephant. An organization is an elephant. Society is an elephant. Each is a whole that is more than the sum of its pieces. Systems thinking contributes to holistic thinking and is an important aspect of it. Systems thinking asserts that the parts of a system are connected and a change in any one element of the system affects the totality. What makes this mysterious at times is understanding just what the parts of the system are and how those parts affect each other.

Let's look at another metaphor. If you have an infection in your hand, you may end up with a temperature. You feel sick all over, even though the problem seems to be in just one part of your body. Moreover, you're thinking about the pain in your hand, so you're distracted, and your emotional well-being is affected, too—you are not in a good mood. Then, you're supposed to shake someone's hand, and you back away because it would be too painful. Your normal interaction with people is affected. You have to explain why you can't shake the person's hand or why you suddenly have a limp handshake, or why you are grimacing.

Steve had a little cut on his thumb, with this slight damage to a tiny portion of one of his digits, he no longer had the capacity to button his own shirt collar. His wife left for work before he did, so Steve either had to go to work looking a little disheveled with an open collar or figure out how to get someone

Suggestions for Action

- With respect to initiatives and challenges, look holistically for existing linkages and connections.
- With respect to initiatives and challenges, look for potential linkages and connections that can be created.
- With respect to initiatives and challenges, look for weak linkages and connections that can be strengthened.
- Create vertical as well as horizontal connections, such as providing an opportunity for eighth-grade teachers to talk with ninth-grade teachers.
- Create connections that cut across interest groups, such as providing an opportunity for groups of students to talk with administrators and board members.

else to button his shirt, which is trickier than it sounds. Suppose someone walks in while his secretary is buttoning his shirt; they're probably going to think something other than, "Oh, Steve must have cut his thumb."

In a holistic world, little things mean a lot. As a child, you may have learned the nursery rhyme: "For want of a nail the shoe was lost. For want of a shoe the horse was lost. For want of a horse the rider was lost. For want of a rider the battle was lost. For want of a battle the kingdom was lost. And all for the want of a horseshoe nail." In this nursery rhyme, the pattern of events and their interconnectedness are clear enough for a child to see. But in the real world, the patterns are not always so clear; sometimes the interconnections occur at an energy level, and they may have a spiritual rather than physical explanation. Synchronicity is one of those mysterious phenomena that can be observed in the physical world even though its roots may lie in a nonvisible spiritual dimension of existence. We understand this idea is speculative, but some leading physicists now believe that our universe actually has eleven dimensions, seven more than the standard four people talk about, including time. We believe that in a holistic world, our thoughts, words, and deeds have spiritual as well as material implications and effects.

THE BUTTERFLY EFFECT AND ITS IMPLICATIONS FOR LEADERS

The Butterfly Effect is beautifully described in James Gleick's book *Chaos*. In it, he tells what happened when Edward Lorenz, a scientist at the Massachusetts Institute of Technology, created a new computer model for long-range weather prediction. Lorenz ran his simulation many times to test its accuracy, and somehow, he kept getting different results. He was confused by that because he thought he was putting the same data in each time and should have gotten identical results. He soon discovered that, initially, he was using data accurate to six decimal places, but that in the subsequent simulations he had rounded the data to three decimal places. He had assumed that rounding the data by one part in a thousand would be of little consequence. Instead, his model showed that a very small change in a single variable in the thousandth place resulted in a vastly different outcome in the predicted weather pattern. In a paper he presented at the annual meeting of the American Association for the Advancement of Science in 1979, he posed this question: "Does the flap of a butterfly's wings in Brazil set off a tornado in Texas?" Subsequent experiments in other nonlinear systems—where relationships are not proportional—demonstrated something that was counterintuitive; namely, that very tiny changes in initial conditions yielded vastly different results down the line. The world is a complex, nonlinear system, and there is now scientific evidence to suggest that in such systems small actions can have big consequences.

People often look to the natural world to discover things about themselves, and the Butterfly Effect holds an important lesson. The smallest things you do can have large effects, both good and bad, so you must be attentive to the little things because they actually do mean a lot. People are inclined to think that some small action is not going to have a big effect, but thanks to the Butterfly Effect, there's compelling evidence that the opposite is true. Being aware that little things have big effects should help you realize how important everyone is. It should help dispel the notion that certain people don't really matter or that what you do doesn't matter because it is just one thing.

What Might This Look Like in Practice?

For months, Paul had been trying to work with a company to develop a partnership. This company would be worth hundreds of thousands of dollars in new revenue to Paul's organization if things played out as planned. While Paul was making progress in this joint venture, a member of his staff mishandled an Internet interaction with the prospective partners in a way that led them to believe she was trying to mislead them. At that point, the company began pulling back from the proposed partnership. One small action in one part of the organization created all sorts of havoc in another. The Butterfly Effect created a typhoon that would take enormous energy to clean up.

Something like this happens in school districts all the time. A secretary treats a visiting parent badly, and the next thing you know, that parent runs for the school board, gets elected, and makes the superintendent's life miserable, all because of some small incident. Any organization can come up with all sorts of examples of how small actions have big outcomes because, ultimately, everything is connected to everything else.

Paul recalls an incident during his Tucson superintendency that caused a group of parents to believe their children's school was unsafe. Even though there was no real basis for the alarm, people's perceptions were running amok, and hysteria reigned. Paul made a tactical decision not to go to the school in the early stages, thinking that would lend credence to the hysteria. Instead, his decision was

Suggestions for Action

- Identify something small that you did that had a larger than anticipated *positive* effect.
- Identify something small that you did that had a larger than anticipated *negative* effect.
- Identify something small that happened to you that had a larger than anticipated *positive* effect.
- Identify something small that happened to you that had a larger than anticipated *negative* effect.
- Identify a policy change in your organization that had a much larger effect than anticipated.
- Identify a personal change that had a much larger effect than anticipated.
- Teach your staff about the Butterfly Effect.
- Ask your staff to alert you to issues or people that might precipitate the Butterfly Effect.

interpreted as being uncaring; even more havoc arose because now people were mad not only about the school but about the superintendent and the district and everything else. The sense grew that nobody cared enough to come down to the school and check out the situation. In making what he thought was a small decision, Paul's action ended up having a big impact, reminding him that it is always harder to put the toothpaste back in the tube once it is out.

The Butterfly Effect contributes to the unpredictability of life, but it also reminds us that what everyone does is important. One vote can change the outcome of an election or a court decision. In 2000, a single vote of the Supreme Court determined who would be the next president of the United States. One person cast the deciding vote, 5 to 4, and our future as a nation unfolded one way instead of another. In a democracy, this dynamic underscores the power of one person. We all affect other people's lives. Contrary to the popular notion that everyone is dispensable, no one is—at least not without some consequence. Leaders strive to maintain some semblance of continuity, but changes in personnel invariably change organizations in both seen and unseen ways.

LEADERS MUST KNOW HOW THE PARTS AND THE WHOLE ARE RELATED

Everything around you is made up of interrelated systems, and if you take a part out of the mix, as we described earlier, like cutting your thumb, or if you don't have a business administrator, or if you can't serve lunch to a thousand kids, what happens? What happens if you don't have electricity, or you don't have a bus, or some other element in the organization is missing? One of the best ways to gain an appreciation of the importance of the parts within an organization is to imagine pulling some part out. What happens when someone who works for you is ill for a prolonged period or someone can't do what he or she is supposed to do? How does that affect others? How does it affect the organization?

In Milton, West Virginia, there's a hand-blown glass factory, Blenko Glass, where they make fine pitchers, bowls, and glass products. It's interesting to go to the factory floor to watch the workers because the men who blow the glass are premier artisans. They have the technique down pat. They put a wad of molten glass on the end of these long pipes and blow into the pipe while they manipulate the molten mass to make whatever they are creating. But if you look at the factory floor, you realize it is not just a bunch of guys with pipes sitting around blowing glass. All these other guys work there. One guy heats the glass to a certain temperature in the furnace and then takes it over to the glassblower. While he's blowing, another guy holds the forms, wooden tools that are used to shape the glass and create the perfect shape for the vase or whatever is being made. After the glass is blown, another guy cuts it off and takes it someplace to be cooled.

They all have different jobs. Some of the jobs are fairly menial, and some are highly skilled, but they are all important. The glassblowers make more money than the others, but if the guy cutting the glass off the pipe doesn't do it right, everything that has happened up to that point doesn't matter. Instead of a beautiful bowl, you have a mess. Every job is critical to the other jobs; they are interrelated and intertwined.

Glass blowing is a great metaphor for organizations: Every job is important; none is insignificant. If you picture people in your organization not being there, and the related work that they do and the contribution that they make not being carried out, you suddenly realize how important they are to you and the others who rely on them. If you don't have somebody with a boiler's license and the law says you can't open a building without someone who has one, or the kids aren't there because you don't have a bus driver, then suddenly all the people with other skills can't use them. In effect, like the Blenko Glass Factory, you can end up with a mess instead of a beautiful piece of hand-blown glass.

Another useful metaphor for understanding the relationship of the part and the whole is human DNA. Something as minute as a single cell among the billions of cells in your body holds within it the blueprint for the whole you. Think about that! It is mind-boggling that a cell from your fingernail or your kidney or your ear actually has within its nucleus a code that can reveal the blueprint for your entire being. Scientists tell us that stem cells not only have the genetic blueprint, they have the potential to actually become a fingernail, or a kidney, or an ear, or any part of us. It is a little bit of a stretch, but this relationship between cells and the whole body is something like the relationship between people and their organization. Teachers have the potential to be a principal or to be a superintendent. Just like a cell, you not only affect the whole but also can grow and evolve into different aspects of the whole.

To the child who is sitting in the classroom, particularly in elementary schools, the teacher is the system. The teacher represents the whole. For most teachers, the principal represents the whole. They know that there is a super-intendent and a school board, and they know some things happen outside of the building, but for most of their day, the person who affects them the most is their principal. In this context, everyone reflects the whole, and everyone represents the whole. One of the keys to a good organization is when everyone is aware of that—when everyone is aware of his or her role in representing the wholeness of the organization.

What Might This Look Like in Practice?

Steve remembers two cashiers who worked in a school cafeteria. One used to help make the kids' days in a positive way: She would smile at each child on the lunch line and make sure that the tray of food that child had selected held something nutritious. She took pride in being a caring adult for each child, the person who wanted to be sure that you were OK and asked how you were feeling. The cashier on one of the other lunch lines was just the opposite. She would scowl at the kids, tell them to hurry up, and often had something negative to say. When kids came out of the cafeteria, depending on which line they were in, they were either smiling or upset, which of course often carried over into the rest of their day. One of these cashiers represented the district in a positive way and had a positive impact. The other reflected poorly on the district and had a negative impact. The negative cashier may have been fulfilling her job from a technical point of view, but from a holistic point of view, she did not reflect the district's caring philosophy, so she was relieved of her position.

Suggestions for Action

- Remember that one of the keys to a successful organization is helping everyone become aware that he or she is part of the whole.
- Highlight stories about the little things that have positive effects on people's lives.
- Tell your staff about the Butterfly Effect and how it can squelch or give wings to children's dreams.
- Foster activities and policies that create a sense of belongingness for both students and staff.
- Share stories that show the interdependence within and among constituencies.
- Use appreciation days and recognition programs to highlight the contributions of everyone in the organization.
- Help people link their hopes and dreams to the hopes and dreams of the organization.

FRACTALS CAN BE A VALUABLE TOOL FOR LEADERS

The notion of a fractal comes from chaos theory, which posits that the universe is made up of repeating patterns, somewhat like the Russian doll sets where you have smaller and smaller replicas of the same doll, each nested inside a bigger one. Size varies, but all of the other aspects—image, coloring, and shape—are repeating patterns. Another example would be looking at the structural pattern of an atom compared to the structural pattern of our solar system. The atom is really a fractal of the solar system in the sense that it has a center or nucleus with ringed energy patterns of electrons moving around it, mirroring the pattern of the sun and planets. According to fractal theory, the same patterns are found in different orders of magnitude going from the very, very tiny to the very, very large. The importance of this concept is that patterns on one scale frequently can tell something about what is found at another scale. Or, from parts of a pattern, the observer may be able to infer what the complete pattern looks like. Parts of things facilitate predictions and generalizations about larger versions of similar patterns.

One of the advantages of living in a holistic world is that there are patterns everywhere. The more those patterns are identified, the easier it is to understand the whole. Pattern recognition—whether at a physical or social level involving people, events, and relationships—makes you more efficient and effective because with partial information; you may be able to discern what's going on before the scale increases or the pattern comes more completely into view. If you can focus on a fractal, you may get an understanding of how these things play out at larger and larger orders of magnitude. The whole notion of pilot-testing is based on that principle. In pilot-testing, you take a fractal of reality, watch it, and if it works, scale it up. Engineers have found limits to scaling because of gravity or the strength of certain materials, but for most intents and purposes, it works quite well. So one practical application of fractals is being able to extrapolate; you see a pattern, and from that you are pretty certain that you know what the rest is going to look like or you know what it is going to look like in a larger form.

Leadership is about connecting the dots, identifying the patterns and enabling others to see them. Leaders may detect patterns that other people don't yet see; they are also open to seeing patterns that others see and open to their perspectives. Leaders see the whole and the parts, the big and the little. The ability to do this is one of the qualities that enable leaders to lead.

Seeing part, leaders can extrapolate the rest, or at least enough to make informed judgments. Some leaders do that intuitively, but we think it would be good training for people in leadership positions to be given experiences in looking at data and partial patterns to learn how to extrapolate and envision the larger or more complete version. Pattern recognition is one of the reasons that leaders can see things early. Successful leaders can recognize fractals and foresee when something may work or become problematic, as those fractals evolve into their larger or more fully developed forms.

A HOLOGRAPHIC PERSPECTIVE IS
A VALUABLE TOOL FOR LEADERS

Holograms are three-dimensional photographs made with the aid of a laser using a process called holography. The images have a fascinating property. If you cut the image into a fractional part, you can use the part to recreate the whole picture. You can cut the hologram up and, no matter how small the parts are, you can still create the whole. The whole always contains its parts, but this is a real world example where the parts actually contain the whole. Instead of the whole being the sum of its parts, it exists within any of its parts. In fact, each and every point in the hologram can be used to create the whole picture, so that all of the points can be thought of as having equal value. Clearly, in a hologram, no one point is more important than any other point.

We see this as a useful metaphor for thinking about the potential of people in an organization. If you think about each person having the inherent qualities that you would like to see in your organization as a whole, that view can trigger an appreciation for every person's value, contribution, and impact on the totality. All you need to do is think of each person as a point in a hologram, which has the capacity to depict the organization as a whole.

The relationship between any point in a hologram and the whole reminds us a little of the notion that each person not only contains the whole but may even be the center of the whole. Scientists have, in fact, tried to find the center of the universe, and they can't. Their experiments seem to find the center wherever they start measuring. In effect, the universe is expanding, and every point in the universe functions like the center. For an analogy, think of the air in a balloon that is being heated. As the air is heated, the balloon expands because the molecules inside the balloon are moving further and further away from each other. Scientists studying the universe have found is that if you take any point on the balloon's surface as the starting point, all of the other points are moving away from it at the same rate. Stars and galaxies are all doing the same thing, moving away from each other at a constant rate. From that perspective, every star functions as the center of the universe. Using the principle of fractals, if it is true for stars, why not people? People tend to think they are the center of the universe. Perhaps it's true. You may not only be the center of your own universe but of the universe as a whole.

THE SPIRITUAL LESSONS OF
ONENESS, UNITY, AND HOLISTIC THINKING

If you see yourself as the center of the universe but you see yourself as disconnected, you behave in one way. If you see yourself as the center of the universe but one who is also connected to the rest of the universe, you behave in a different way. Our perspective is that everyone is interconnected. We hope that you see or will come to see yourself in that light. Everything that you do, directly or indirectly, impacts on the rest of us, which really gets to the heart of the spiritual lesson of oneness. It is a matter of being a productive positive force as opposed to being a destructive negative force because if you don't see yourself as someone who is at one with things, you behave in a very different way than if you see yourself as connected to others and the universe.

Part of your responsibility as a leader is to help people understand and appreciate the unity and the connectedness that exists within whatever organization or family unit they are a part of. One of the keys to successful leadership is understanding the spiritual lesson of unity and then sharing that understanding so that other people get it—to the point that it becomes part of their belief system and their value system, and they can then see each other as part of that unity. The lesson of unity is not just an arrow of understanding that goes from the leader to all the other people; rather, it is an array of arrows that go from every person to every other person.

The pattern reminds Steve of his first week as superintendent of a new school district that had ten schools. He proudly announced that he could find his way from his office to every one of the schools and get back—and the schools were not easy to find. One member of the staff responded to Steve's pronouncement by saying that was a very good initial step, but the real test was to get from any one of the schools to all of the other schools. Steve could see his celebration had been premature because he had a limited perspective. The task was 10 times more complicated than he first realized. He had learned 20 routes where he really needed to learn close to 200.

This same idea is a fractal of the lines of connection among people in an organization. For example, if you have 100 people in your organization, there is a potential connection from each person to every one of the other 99 people. You could picture each person as the center and draw arrows to and from the other 99, and you could see these as potential lines of energy connecting everyone to everyone else. With e-mail, you can have holistic patterns of communication within every organization. When used appropriately, this can be one way of helping people gain a sense of unity and connectedness.

Martin Luther King, Jr., spoke eloquently about the notion of unity and connectedness in his speech from the Birmingham jail when he said,

> In a real sense all life is interrelated. All men are caught in an inescapable network of mutuality, tied into a single garment of destiny. Whatever affects one directly, affects all indirectly. I can never be what I ought to be until you are what you ought to be, and you can never be what you ought to be until I am what I ought to be. This is the interrelated structure of reality.

Dr. King's words convey the essence of holistic thinking. He reminds us that all people are connected and what affects one, affects all. Good leaders are not only inspired by such words—they try to live by them.

One of the spiritual lessons you can draw from Dr. King is that when you act on something, or when you fail to act, you are not acting on one thing—you are acting on everything. That is true for better or worse. Whether you act in a positive or negative way, you affect all the things that are interconnected. It's good to be mindful of this underlying unity even though it is not always readily apparent.

Steve experienced this firsthand when he and his family visited the island of Maui and went on a hike in the rain forest with a naturalist. On the way to a beautiful waterfall, the group followed a trail through a bamboo forest, 60-foot-high bamboo trees only inches apart, as far as the eye could see—thousands of them, or so Steve thought. The naturalist explained that while above ground they seemed to be seeing thousands of separate trees, in fact, below ground, a single root system connected all of them. The appearance of separateness was illusory. In fact, this was one enormous tree rather than thousands of separate trees, but this was not apparent to anyone walking through the forest who didn't have a deep understanding of the true nature of the underlying reality.

As a leader, you can model holistic thinking by reminding people that they are a part, a truly important part, of something bigger than themselves. Not only are they a part of the whole, but the whole is even greater than the sum of its parts. By working together synergistically and holistically, people can increase their power and capacity to achieve goals and have a shared sense of purpose. Holistic thinking promotes a sense of unity within an organization, as do initiatives that help create a sense of identity and a shared culture. When people work together in unity, you begin to see the real power of community emerge. An interesting play on words reveals that *community* can be created from *common* and *unity*. Communities are powerful instruments for health, support, purpose, and affirmation. You get that only through a sense of unity. When there is a lack of common ground and a lack of mutual feeling for each other, community suffers. On the other hand, when a sense of unity is tied to a holistic perspective, communities can create positive outcomes.

What Might This Look Like in Practice?

When Paul was working in Princeton, he and the other administrators participated in a workshop where they were all given a reading to do and a test to take based on the reading. It was challenging to find the answers to some of the questions. After each person did the test individually, the group had to come to an agreement on which answer the group would put down. Then they graded it. They found that, in every instance, the group score was higher than the highest score of any individual within the group. In every case, the group—the whole—was more powerful than the sum of the parts.

Paul always loved that exercise because it brings home in a concrete way that the whole can be greater than the sum of its parts. People may say it or hear it, but most of the time, they don't believe it. At most, they believe that the whole is equal to the sum of its parts. Yet a synergistic effect can be created that elevates and magnifies the power of the whole compared to its individual parts or the sum of those parts.

> ### Suggestions for Action
>
> - Create activities and policies that foster *a sense of identity* within the organization.
> - Create activities and policies that foster *a shared culture* within the organization.
> - Create activities and policies that foster *a sense of community* within the organization.
> - Remind people that they are part of something that is greater than any one of us.
> - Cultivate an appreciation for the power of synergy.
> - Encourage people in the organization to think holistically.

Some of the power of the whole being greater than the sum of the parts has to do with energy. In this case, the parts are people who in and of themselves are relatively static, but when people are brought together in a collaborative atmosphere, a dynamic is created from the interaction that increases the flow of energy within the group. By bringing people together in productive and positive ways, leaders can unleash a reservoir of untapped energy within their organizations.

SUMMARY

In a highly specialized world, people rarely think holistically or consider the underlying unity and connectedness of life. These are empowering concepts that you can model and foster in your organization. You can talk about them and bring them into the consciousness of other people, and in so doing actually contribute to their affect. You can do something to foster this principle by the way you bring people together and also by the stories you tell about what you are doing and why. If you tell stories that involve unity, collective action, and holistic thinking, you can expand the number of people in your organization who share and benefit from that view.

NOTE

1. Dialogue is not the same as talking or having a conversation. Dialogue involves attentive listening—listening deeply with respect and extended wait time, as each person contributes to the dialogue. Deep listening brings out the best of what each person has to offer and allows you to tap into your unconscious as well as your conscious knowledge. Dialogue begins with an evocative question such as, "What does this look like from the vantage point of our constituents?" Someone may record or takes notes on each person's key points. The notes are compiled and shared and can then be used to build consensus. We used a version of this process to co-create the content for this book.

The Principle
of Openness

Openness is a state of mind, an attitude toward people, ideas, and circumstances. It is the key to our growth as human beings. People are thought of as being generally open or closed, and so are organizations and societies. A person's degree of openness may fluctuate; you may be more open in some aspects of your life than others, or more open at some times in your life than others. It is not easy to be open because it makes you feel vulnerable and may, in fact, increase your vulnerability.

Openness is complex—openness to whom, openness to what, and under what circumstances? Openness involves letting things in, especially things you don't want to hear, and letting things out, as in openly speaking your truth, especially when it is not popular or good politics.

We subscribe to the notion that enlightened leaders strive to evolve in the direction of openness. Leaders should strive to open their minds to see as many possibilities as they can. They should strive to open their hearts to feel compassion, empathy, and love. And they should strive to open their spirits to the full expression of who they really are. These are lofty goals, but openness happens bit by bit, moment by moment, choice by choice.

When you model openness as a leader, you begin to influence your organization to develop a climate of openness. People know whether they are in an open climate or a closed one. Creativity thrives in open climates—freedom thrives—and there is more joy and spontaneity. Open systems are organic, they grow and evolve; whereas closed systems are stifling, they stagnate and wither.

When you're not open in areas where you need to be more open, the world tends to let you know—there is a natural feedback system. Ironically, you can be open or closed to the feedback that is telling you to be more open, more flexible. You can always close the door to openness, but there is usually a price—your difficulties increase or your pain increases, and you may blame others or external events for this. It has been our experience that the last place most people look for the causes contributing to their difficulties is within themselves.

More than 20 years ago, when Steve's children were ages 10 and 5, his family system wasn't working well. He blamed his kids, and he blamed his wife. He was a busy superintendent doing what busy superintendents do. He wondered why his wife and children couldn't just get along and treat each other well. Steve invited his brother Adam, a psychotherapist, to study the family dynamics and tell him what the problem was and how to resolve it. After watching the family interact for a day, Adam was ready with his analysis of the situation. Boy, was Steve in for a surprise. Steve himself was the problem, Adam said. Wow! Steve didn't see that one coming. He could have questioned Adam's competence—using the old, discredit-the-source approach. But a part of Steve was open to hearing Adam's message, and more important, a part of Steve was open to changing his behavior.

This is a story with a happy ending. The family indeed got better because when one part of a system changes—in this case, Steve in his role as husband and father—it affects the other parts. In this case, his wife and children began treating each other differently, but this happened only because Steve was open to change of the toughest kind—changing his own behavior. Rather than demanding that someone else change, Steve experienced an important life lesson on the power of openness and got to see the positive ripple effects of an open mind and an open heart. The hardest place to start the journey toward openness is with yourself. This is an ongoing, lifelong journey, but we truly believe that for those who are open to openness, the results are well worth the investment.

OPENNESS IS AN IMPORTANT PRINCIPLE FOR LEADERS

We often refer to the issue of openness because, in many ways, it is the prerequisite that allows the other spiritual principles of leadership to come forward. People are so different from each other in terms of where they fall on the continuum of openness. Where you fall on that continuum has a lot to do with the quality of your own life because, generally, you either don't let in much or you let in a great deal. By not allowing things in, you close yourself off from all sorts of potential connections and magic. On the other hand, if you are open, then synchronicity can happen, connections can be made, your connection to your higher self can happen—all those things can come about by being on the more open end of the continuum. To us, openness is also a prerequisite for almost any kind of a fulfilled life. For leaders, it becomes even more critical because, without openness, you are closing off your organization and the people you work with—not just yourself—and you are creating a dynamic that is extremely unhealthy. You have to work at openness. As you nurture that in yourself as a leader, you open up your organization to greater possibilities.

Openness is one of those spiritual principles that are fundamental, but the tough question is openness to what? The number of things you can finish that sentence with is really extraordinary: openness to people, openness to life experiences, openness to ideas, openness to letting people know you and to knowing yourself, openness to change, openness to growth, openness to criticism, openness to the Divine. We could just keep extending that list. The field of what you may or may not be open to is vast. The real question is not just "Are you open?" but rather "To what extent are you open?" The continuum runs from not being open at all to being completely open. In some areas, people may be very open, perhaps in their relationships with others, but in another area, such as dealing with new ideas, they may be much less so. Imagine a vast array of doorways, each open to varying degrees in every dimension of your life. You decide when and under what circumstances you will open or close each doorway, and to what degree.

The spiritual principles of leadership are like gateways of possibilities, which imply openness because you can't go through a gateway without opening it. You can't go through a door without it being open, unless you have higher powers than we have developed. You've got to have the mind-set of being open, and then you've got to have the willingness to walk through the opening. A certain level of trust and courage is involved in all this. Trust itself is inextricably connected to openness, where each quality can reinforce and serve as the wellspring for the other. Love is another spiritual principle that comes about through openness, where fear closes everything down, including love. Negative feelings and anger also close things down. *When things are closed nothing flows.* For anything to flow, even blood, the channels have to be open. A blockage in the bloodstream or air passage can kill you. Likewise, in an organizational structure, if you have individuals blocking and closing things down, it creates an unhealthy situation. From a spiritual point of view, a closed mind and closed heart can create a blockage that cuts you off from your connection to the Divine and from your sense of possibilities; an open mind and open heart have the opposite effect.

It is your responsibility as a leader to model what you believe. If you believe in the principle of openness, you must model it in as many ways as possible. If you want the people in your organization to be open to growth and change and to new experiences and ideas, then you need to model it yourself. Doing so demonstrates that openness is a valued quality, an attribute that you respect and appreciate, not only as a valuable quality but as a fundamental quality for being effective.

What Might This Look Like in Practice?

There was a time in Steve's career when he was getting some consistent feedback that he was not doing a good job of balancing the needs of the organization with the needs of the people within it. The feedback was that his decisions were too heavily weighted in terms of the needs of the organization and not weighted enough on the people side. Because he was getting that message from a number of sources he respected, he acknowledged—and this was tough—that the feedback was accurate, that the problem was not perception or communication but his leadership style. He was then faced with the decision of what he was going to do about it. He could have said, "OK, that's who I am, you'll have to live with it; after all, I'm the superintendent." Instead, he realized that he needed to make a shift toward the human side if he wanted to be more effective. First, he openly declared his intention to use this problem as a growth opportunity, and he publicly declared a personal goal to change his behavior. He told the staff, "There are some things that clearly must be decided in favor of the overall needs of the organization. But in the future, when decisions fall in the gray zone, I will come down in favor of the human side rather than the organizational side of the equation. Now that you know my intention, I invite you to watch my behavior and let me know how I'm doing."

Steve modeled openness by creating a climate where criticism could be expressed and not stifled. He modeled openness in accepting a problem and committing to resolving it even though it required change on his part. And he modeled openness by publicly acknowledging both the problem and his intention to resolve it. Finally, he modeled openness by creating a feedback loop to monitor his progress. As a result, Steve was able to make a shift in his style and create a much better balance in the way he functioned as a leader.

Another reason leaders need to be advocates of openness is that it fosters creativity. Part of the creative process has to do with openness because, unless you've got the spigots turned wide open, you can't access creative thinking. In today's world, creative leaders are needed more than ever before, leaders who have access to everything that is out there for their organizations. Openness becomes a

Suggestions for Action

- Identify some aspect of your *professional* life where you would like to be more open.
- Identify some aspect of your *personal* life where you would like to be more open.
- Identify some issue or initiative for your organization where you can demonstrate openness to the ideas of others.
- Identify some area where you are open to taking a risk to achieve a worthy goal.
- Use the principle of intention to help manifest openness in the identified areas.
- Use the principle of attention to help manifest openness in the identified areas.
- Use the principle of a holistic perspective to help manifest openness in the identified areas.

prerequisite for any kind of creative expression on the part of the leader as well as the internal health and flow of the organization.

As with many things, it is easier to talk about openness than to practice it. Even if you consciously want to move in the direction of openness, some things that prevent or inhibit openness may be operating at an unconscious level. If you want to be open to something but can't seem to align your actions with your intentions, you may have to look at yourself at a deeper level to figure out where the blockage is rooted. Often, it is rooted in conscious or unconscious fear.

THE SPIRITUAL ASPECTS OF OPENNESS

Openness involves a certain level of faith and trust, which we see as fundamental spiritual qualities. From a spiritual perspective, you must have faith that a certain amount of bounty will come to you, your organization, and your relationships. It is also important that you have some sense of divine connection. In his professional life, Paul has often taken actions, made decisions, and moved his organization in certain directions that were risky and made some people nervous. People asked him, "How can you do that?" The answer is by believing deep down that ultimately the Universe works toward good and, that by setting positive things in motion, positive things will happen. It is by being open to the possibilities that are out there and not being afraid of them. We see a direct connection between openness and spirituality.

What Might This Look Like in Practice?

We see spirituality as a way of being. When you act in a caring way, a way that uplifts others and brings out the best in them, you are being spiritual. When you deal with people in the workplace who have done you damage or created problems, and you continue to be accepting and open to their contributions, you are being spiritual. It is fairly easy to turn off on people, particularly when they have been either mean to you or damaging or just stupid. You might assume that what you've seen is as good as it gets. If you are truly open, you will continue to listen and accept contributions with the belief that change is possible. That is hard for a lot of people to do, but if you are operating with a spirit of openness, you accept people's contributions, try to understand their thought patterns, and continue to look for their possibilities.

Paul once had a high school principal who was ineffective and somewhat nasty. Some people wanted Paul to fire this principal because of his history of problems. Paul thought he saw redeeming qualities in the person, so he put him in a different situation, an elementary school. The pressure that he was experiencing as a high school principal was taken away, and Paul believed that as a result, the man might behave differently. That is exactly what happened. Because

Paul remained open to this principal's possibilities, he finished his career successfully at an elementary school where people actually revered him, while just a few years earlier, he was reviled. Paul salvaged not only the person but also the situation for the organization. We believe that people are fundamentally good. The challenge is to act on that belief in situations where their goodness is yet to be revealed.

Another element in the preceding story is that the principal not only resisted Paul, he also worked to undermine him. Paul had to be sufficiently open to get past that and say, "It's not about me, it's not about our relationship, it's about the greater good." There is enough of the warrior in Paul for him to hit back, following the adage: When attacked, react. He chose not to do it because he had seen qualities in this principal that perhaps even the principal himself had forgotten. Paul believed that the anger and the nastiness this person displayed resulted from the pain he was experiencing. Paul thought, "If I could remove the pain, his behavior will change." Paul made a series of choices—all of them were toward remaining open. At any point, Paul could have chosen to close and remove this person from the organization. Openness is not just a single act; it is a series of acts, a journey. It is a constant mind-set of keeping possibilities open—you are dealing with moving targets, and you have to keep recommitting to that sense of openness throughout the process.

To us, the ultimate connection between openness and spirituality is openness to God. If you start with a belief in God—belief itself is a form of openness—then the exercise of that belief is allowing the Divine to guide you, to come into your life and support you, and to help you grow into the best version of yourself. One spiritual aspect of openness is trying to remain open to your connection with the Divine. We count ourselves among those who believe that every human being has a spark of the Divine. From that perspective, being open to other people is a spiritual act, or at least a spiritual mind-set. We believe in a dynamic universe that is evolving as human beings evolve, through an ongoing interactive process. Without openness, there can be no interaction. From our perspective then, whether we are interacting with the environment, with people, or with our higher selves or divine aspect, or with the Divine directly, we are expressing different aspects of the relationship between spirituality and openness.

ENLIGHTENED LEADERS CREATE OPEN SYSTEMS

One way that leaders can create open systems is by being open themselves. You have to *walk the talk* by demonstrating to other people that you are indeed open. Open leaders create open systems by being tight on the goals they set but loose on the ways to achieve them. This is an example of the loosely coupled system described by Peters and Waterman in their best-selling book *In Search of*

Excellence. You want to be clear about where you are trying to go but open about giving people wide latitude in creating options for getting there, as opposed to dictating both the ends and the means. In doing so, you help people to grow and to experience each other in positive ways.

What Might This Look Like in Practice?

In summer 2004, Paul's organization held a board meeting based on a new governing structure. Paul and his officers were moving through the agenda they had planned when they faced an insurrection at the end of the first day. New board members didn't understand their role, and they expected certain things to be happening that weren't. The organization's president showed a great deal of openness by saying, "Look, we'll change the agenda starting tomorrow morning. We will change the agenda to address the issues that you think are important." The insurrection was over. Everybody said, "Oh, OK, cool."

The next day was spent talking about the things that the new board wanted to talk about. Paul and the officers cleared up some areas of confusion, and when the governing board left, they felt they'd had a great meeting where a lot had been accomplished. Had there been less openness, Paul and his officers would have had a real nightmare on their hands. This was a case where there was instant feedback, and the officers responded in an open manner.

According to systems theory, an open system has a feedback loop—information goes out into the system and then comes back, there is some form of reaction and necessary adjustment, and then information goes back out again. There is a continual inflow and outflow of information, the communication is open, and the flow is in two directions. As a leader, you can create structures that either facilitate two-way, ongoing communication or foster one-way communication where barriers make it difficult to go from one level in an organization to another. The more easily information can flow in both directions and between levels, the more open the system is. Leaders can also provide experiences for people that will widen their horizons and help them become more open. The more open those people become, the more open the system becomes.

Steve recalls listening to an interview on National Public Radio in which the guest described a program that helped students become more open through service learning. As a result of their experiences working in nursing homes, the high school students changed their preconceptions about what older people were like and about what it would be like to be with them. The students' fears and misgivings were replaced by feelings of empathy and compassion and a sense of fulfillment. The high school students also worked with preschool children. They learned how young children behave and how to interact with them. As a result of these experiences, the high school students became more open to new ways of thinking and new ways of being.

Leaders can do that for students and staff alike by supporting those individuals who are open to experiencing new roles, relationships, responsibilities, and challenges. Creating experiences that allow people to grow and try something new can result in having them develop a more open perspective, especially if those experiences are positive. You can't predict whether people will respond to new experiences by becoming more open or by closing down. Nonetheless, your role as a leader is to give them the opportunities and to provide encouragement and support along the way.

Sometimes leaders have to give people a safety line to help them to be open to something new. Steve recalls a master fifth-grade teacher who was content to working with her own students in a self-contained class setting that included a limited amount of team teaching. Steve thought this gifted teacher was well suited to become the coordinator of the district's elementary gifted program, where she could not only mentor gifted students but also serve as a role model to other teachers. Steve talked to her about taking the new position when it opened, but she respectfully declined. She was not open to a change. Secure and successful in the world she had created, she was not ready to venture into a new and different role.

As superintendent, Steve was in a position to provide her with a safety line. Steve told her that he understood her reluctance but that he was confident she would find this new role fulfilling, that it would allow her to use her creative talents with a larger number of students and teachers. Steve asked her to try the new position for one year. If, after that time, she still wanted to return to her previous assignment, she could do so. Steve put his assurance in writing. With her safety line in hand, the teacher accepted the new assignment. As is turned out, the teacher did find her new role more rewarding, and she never exercised the option to use her safety line.

Suggestions for Action

- Model openness.
- Employ open, honest communications.
- Use electronic mail to establish instantaneous two-way communication at all levels of the organization.
- Create transparency in terms of what you are doing and why.
- Create transparency in terms of where you hope to be going as an organization.
- Create transparency in terms of the major issues the organization is dealing with.
- Create transparency by letting people know what is under consideration and providing some legitimate process for review and input.
- If there is a crisis or impending problem, call people together and say, "Here are the facts as best we know them."
- If there is a crisis or impending problem, explain how the organization can handle it, giving people a sense of hope, but being as transparent as possible.
- Leaders of organizations in the public sector should make it easy for the public to access information, including budgets, on the organization's Web site.

When Steve wanted to introduce a radically new type of schedule with much longer periods for high school classes in a district where he was superintendent, he give teachers an opportunity to spend time with other teachers who had already experienced teaching in 80- rather than 40-minute periods. Consequently, they became more open to an idea that initially they were closed about. These are examples of how a leader can create opportunities to build openness in others. Leaders can do so even when confronted with an initial reaction that is closed rather than open, which is often the case.

Bringing in new people—new blood—into an organization is another way of fostering a dynamic system, which is almost by definition an open system, one that's continually changing and adapting to internal and external circumstances. New people can provide an infusion of new ideas and vitality if the overall culture is an open one. It creates a flow. The opposite of this is a stagnant system where there is virtually no openness and no growth. An organization needs not only new people but also different kinds of people. When people come from different places, perspectives, and circumstances, they must address those differences, and this has contributed to greater openness in the organizations we have served, as well as in the larger society. It is one of the great values of public education.

LEADERS MUST BE OPEN TO MANY THINGS

First and foremost, leaders must be open to change. People say there are two things you can count on: death and taxes. We would like to add change—you just can't stop it. The universe is a dynamic, ever-changing place at every level—the atom, the cell, the person, the community, the society—wherever you look, the one thing that is always occurring is change. Obviously, the rate of change varies, and so does the degree of change, but change itself is a constant. As a result, having an open attitude toward change is fundamental to both life and leadership.

What Might This Look Like in Practice?

Being open means being willing to make the changes in yourself that are needed to make you effective. Leaders also have to be open to changing conditions. What worked or what was appropriate at one time, in one organization, or in one situation may be terribly inappropriate in another case. School boards and superintendents don't always recognize this in their dealings with each other. People are brought in to meet one set of conditions, but once those are addressed successfully, the organization faces a different set of conditions, and the leader's inability to make the shift can be a problem.

For example, a board hired Paul to do certain things, and by all accounts, he was successful. The next board came in with a different set of expectations, expecting him to behave in a different manner. He had to decide whether to adjust or move on. For the good of the organization, he chose to adjust, even though it wasn't necessarily something he wanted to do. This dynamic is a constant challenge for leaders because, as the Zen teaching says, "You never step in the same river twice." Everything is always moving so if you are not being open to the changing conditions around you, you could be open today and look closed tomorrow; openness always takes place in a context.

When an organization has an open culture, people are encouraged to come forward with new ideas and initiatives. Leaders need to be open to considering the ideas, suggestions, and concerns that come to them—to give them some thought and not just to dismiss them out of hand. You should consider the options others suggest as well as the options that you can envision. Remember the rule about being alert to guidance and help from the Universe: If something shows up two or three times in your life, pay attention! The Universe encourages you to move in certain directions, but you must be open to the information you are getting—at some level, the Universe is trying to help you to be the best you can be and do the best you can do. Issues that provoke change are not always pleasant. It may seem easier to resist the information or suggestions or needs swirling around you rather than make a shift.

Also, it can be hard to embrace the pain you associate with change or the pain of new ideas that may knock you off your pedestal. It can be hard to embrace the pain of rejection when the path you are on is not the right path.

Above all, leaders need to be open to others. There's a stereotype that an only child can be selfish and refuse to share toys freely. To some extent, everyone is an only child. People come into the world alone, and they learn to play well with others in tandem with physical growth and maturity. To a large extent, society and organizations are dependent on people having the ability to play well with each other. This requires being open to other people.

Leaders also need to be open to the paradoxical nature of life—the fact that many times two and two makes something other than four. Things don't necessarily add up. Ten plus four doesn't always add up to fourteen—on an analog clock ten plus four equals two. There isn't always a right and a wrong answer. In many cases, a number of possibilities are equally right and equally wrong. Being open to that is difficult for most people, and especially for leaders who are supposed to know what the right path is. Our experience is that no single path is the right one, and sometimes there is no path at all. As a leader, you spend most of your time cutting through the underbrush trying to make a path where there isn't any. Sometimes you choose to go in the direction that gets you there faster, and sometimes you take the circuitous, scenic route. But you have to be open to the fact that sometimes on the scenic route you see things you needed to see. If you hadn't taken that route, you wouldn't know those things.

Leaders need to be open to surprise and magic—to knowing you will *not* know what is going to happen, that sometimes wonderful things can happen when you least expect it. Answers will come to you from the most unlikely of places, and you need to have your eyes and ears open, and your brain willing to accept that.

Leaders must be open to the fact that the world often appears unjust. If you are looking for tidiness and completion, for things always to work out the way you think they should, then you've got a problem. You have to be open to the fact that you may not know what is best in the long run and that while things seem to be unjust at a given moment in time, that moment may be just one step on the path to a more just conclusion. You have to be open to that possibility.

Not only your eyes and ears but also your heart, mind, and spirit need to be kept open. When you do this, you have more channels active for processing your life experiences. The principle of openness comes into play in terms of whether you are sensitive to the information you are receiving and whether you respond to that information in an open or closed way. So you need to work at opening all of those aspects of yourself. When your heart, mind, or spirit is closed, the Universe will let you know. When your heart is closed and too hard, or your ideas are too rigid, or you are not seeing what is right in front of you, or you are closed off from your own spirit, you will get lots of signals. What do you do with that information? Again, the ongoing feedback loop applies. You can be open or closed to the information that you receive about not being open enough. Just as change is an ongoing process, the degree of openness in all these channels varies with time and circumstance in a dynamic process. Maybe you were fairly open last year, but this year, due to specific circumstances, you've become less open. You can't say, "Well, I was open last year

Suggestions for Action

- Model behaviors that show you are continually working at your own growth and development.
- Look for and create opportunities to foster other people's growth.
- Be open to the lessons you are receiving, even if they involve some degree of discomfort.
- Acknowledge your own fallibility and be willing to say, "I was wrong."
- Be willing to say, "My assumption is no longer valid, and I need to adjust my thinking to meet a different set of conditions."
- Follow Richard Farson's advice in *He Who Makes the Most Mistakes Wins*, where he says leaders must be willing to express openness about areas where they have erred rather than trying to portray themselves as near perfect.
- Be mindful that making mistakes is what allows you to learn, grow, and move forward in becoming a better leader.

so I don't have to be open this year." As you process the events in your life, your degree of openness creates consequences for you and those you lead.

Your degree of openness is always in flux. It's like a door that doesn't hang quite level, so gradually it closes on its own. That happens a lot. You may have your moments of clarity where you're moving along, you're open, you're taking in what's being offered, and then one day, you wake up and realize something happened—you're just not doing that any more. So you have to remain open to the fact that you're not always going to be open. It's not a linear progression. Sometimes you move forward, and sometimes you move back. Sometimes, you're more open, and sometimes you close up. Events sometimes may cause you to draw in. You can look back at your own life and recall moments of great openness, and other moments when you were pretty closed down. The key is to be aware as much as possible of how open you are and to remind yourself that if you are not open enough, you need to work on it and move forward on that front. Just be aware that you may not always do as well as you'd like to do in being open. That's just the way it works. It's not a straight line of progress where you are more open this year than you were last year, and next year, you will be still more open. By working at it, however, you can increase your tendency toward openness so it becomes a lot easier to recapture.

OPENING YOUR HEART AND MIND

Most people would say they are or would like to be open-minded. If you asked if they would like an open heart, we suspect there would be a mixed reaction; some people associate an open heart with being vulnerable and being hurt emotionally. When we refer to an open mind and open heart, we mean open in the sense of being able to take in and optimally process the full range of life's experiences. But we also mean open in the sense of being able to express who you really are both intellectually and emotionally.

What Might This Look Like in Practice?

Paul often gives talks on the relationship between school boards and superintendents. He likes to give his audience his ten commandments for school board/superintendent relations. One of the commandments is: It's all personal. People in organizations have a tendency to say what happens isn't personal, but it is—and it should be. In fact, the way you open your heart is to make everything personal.

As a leader, Paul tries to get to know the people he is leading, and not just by name or by whether they are good at doing X or Y. He wants to know: Do they have kids? Do they have families? What are their backgrounds? Do they have hobbies? What do they like to do when they are not working? When you do that and you get to know people on a personal basis, they become human. Besides having information about them, you begin to see them as fully rounded human beings. Likewise, when you are talking with people, you reveal things about yourself so that you become human to them as well. When two people meet and get to know each other, there is an opportunity for their hearts to connect naturally. If you don't allow that to happen, then it is very difficult to relate to others with an open heart.

What can you do to open your hearts and minds, as opposed to the things that life does to you? You can be proactive in trying to become more open-minded and open-hearted, or you can be reactive. When you are reactive, you still have a choice of remaining either closed or open. Opening your heart can be stimulated by internal as well as external forces. Working on yourself from within becomes a process of wanting to have a heart that shows greater feeling, more compassion, more forgiveness, more trust, more generosity, more understanding, and other qualities associated with a big, open heart. Being more open-minded means being more willing to try new things, being more tolerant, and being more interested in new ideas and thinking that differs from your own. If you want to be more open, you can do some things to move in that direction, in the same way that if you want to be healthier physically, you can do things that impact your health, such as exercise, a good diet, and plenty of rest. If you want to acquire certain attributes, such as being more open, you can use your intention and attention to move in that direction.

We believe that life pushes us to have open hearts and open minds and that people are constantly getting feedback in the areas where their hearts or their minds aren't open enough. What do you do with that feedback? You either close down tighter, or you begin to say, "Hmmm, perhaps I need to make a change." For example, Steve has a friend with significant physical problems. From time to time, Steve talks to him about different types of exercise that he might do to help resolve some of those problems, exercises that would begin to move his friend's body in the direction of health. His friend's attitude is: "Because I have physical problems, I can't exercise." This friend has a mind-set that exercise is not an option for him, that it might be helpful to others but not him. Steve hoped he would say, "I appreciate your level of concern, and perhaps, I could take a short walk as a way of moving forward with some modest exercise, or I can walk around the house, taking 10 steps today and 11 steps tomorrow." Instead, his friend's attitude was, "Don't be intrusive; let me be. It's my body, not yours. I have to live with the consequences, and I'll make my own decisions." That's true, but to Steve, his friend has closed his mind to new possibilities and is holding fast to a rigid position, despite information and concern coming from someone who cares about his well-being.

Paul was very close to someone whose disabilities were emotional rather than physical; that person lived a very closed life and exhibited exactly the same behaviors as Steve's friend: "Leave me alone. I don't want to be able to travel. I don't want to be able to go out in public. I'm happy being closed in my little environment." Whereas Steve's friend is closed in his thinking, Paul's friend is closed in her feelings, but the phenomenon was the same.

On the other hand, we all know people who are far along in the process of opening their minds and hearts, people who are continually striving to become a better person. Those closest to Steve see him as one of these people. Steve continually looks at people around him for role models. He sees certain people who are extraordinarily gracious, or who are giving or loving or kind. When someone has been kind, caring, giving, or loving toward him, he then says to himself, "I really like the way that makes me feel." Or he sees the way a child or a staff member responds to a kind person. He says to himself, "I want to be more like that." So he is actually trying to become a better person by emulating others.

Here is a personal example of this process. Steve's daughter-in-law had a birthday coming up, and Steve wondered what he should give her. Steve and his wife generally give their children monetary gifts for their birthdays, so it was really a question of how much money should he and his wife give their daughter-in-law. One part of Steve said, "She's pretty new to the family. We don't have a very close relationship at this point, so let's not get carried away. Maybe we should do something modest, and then in the future when we have a much closer relationship, then perhaps I'll be more generous." One little voice went off in his mind saying that. Another little voice said, "Now wait a minute. You've been married for 35 years. Whenever you had a birthday, did your wife's parents treat you any differently than they treated their own daughter?" He realized immediately that from Day 1, his wife's parents had treated him and their daughter equally, as though they loved them both the same. He remembered how wonderful that felt, and he then consciously tried to behave in a way that justified their love.

Having had that experience, Steve knew that whatever he was doing for his own son was the right thing to do for his son's new wife. And so that's what he did. His new daughter-in-law was almost blown away by their generosity. The gift was a powerful message that Steve and his wife were treating her like a daughter. Steve was not trying to buy love or affection. He just wanted to do the right thing. If his heart had truly been open, he would have known the right thing to do and wouldn't have been confused. Steve's mind and heart weren't on the same wavelength so he did not have clarity. There were many options for deciding on the right course of action. Steve opted to look back at what he considered to be a positive role model to remind himself of the way a person with an open heart—namely, his own father-in-law—behaved in a similar situation.

Steve's gift to his daughter-in-law involved a journey from conditional to unconditional love. To some extent, the journey toward openness is the journey toward unconditional love. When you start attaching conditions, you start shutting down. When you strip those conditions away, you become more open.

An open mind reflects flexibility and a willingness to change. An open heart allows you to make those changes with a spirit of generosity and love. Paul had a chance to practice the principle of openness when he became engaged and invited his fiancé to move in with him. This meant converting *his* place and space to *their* place and space. Paul fills up all his available space with stuff, interesting and beautiful stuff but lots of it. First, Paul had to open his mind to the prospect of letting go of a lot of stuff. Then, he physically had to create open space to make room for his fiancé's stuff by actually letting go of some things. At the same time, he had exactly the same experience in his office because the organization was moving to a new location with more limited space. He had to get rid of stuff at the office as well.

Paul had an open mind toward the message he was getting from the Universe. He just viewed it as the Universe's way of helping him shed the need to have so much stuff and learn a new quality, which is to be able to let go of things. Paul's experience is a metaphor for openness in general. When you are open, you are not bogged down by a bunch of stuff—whether it's emotional stuff or intellectual stuff or actual physical stuff. The more weighted down you are, the more difficult it is to be open.

Earlier we pointed out that in your journey to become more open-minded and open-hearted you can be either proactive or reactive. We shared several examples of being

Suggestions for Action

- Be mindful that opening your heart and mind often requires taking substantial risk.
- Be compassionate and avoid hardening of the "hearteries."
- Surround yourself with people who think differently.
- Remember that in hope-based cultures, the heart begins to open.
- Move your organization in the direction of hope and away from fear.
- Create an uplifting, joyful environment that is full of opportunity, goodwill, and caring.
- Create opportunities for people to get to know each other.
- Look for informal opportunities to get to know your staff and for them to get to know you.
- Model forgiveness and a sense of trust.
- Listen to your heart.

proactive but also, and perhaps more often than not, people end up reacting. Life happens, and then you react; certainly, your reaction side needs to be open. This is difficult because when you are reacting, you may mirror the action that is happening to you. For example, if the initiating event is caused by someone who is not very open, who perhaps does not have your best outcome in their heart and mind, it is easy for you to fall to that level. Nevertheless, even when you are reacting to people and situations, you have to be proactive to maintain an open mind and an open heart.

Life wants you to have an open heart and mind because it is essential to your own growth. You cannot grow when your heart and mind are closed. Regardless of the extent to which your heart and mind are open, life seems to push you to become increasingly more open. How open you are to the process of becoming still more open seems to determine how easy or difficult the process is for you. Sometimes it takes heartache or even heartbreak to open up. Sometimes it can be as easy as a whisper from someone you love or admire, or as sweet and gentle as the love in a child's eyes.

HOW OPENNESS MAXIMIZES GROWTH AND CREATIVITY

You can't go somewhere when you're all weighted down, and people are often weighted down by all sorts of stuff—biases, preconceptions, prejudices, anger, resentment. You name it, and people have got those rocks in their pocket all the time. So part of openness is casting away a lot of that stuff. It is taking the weight off so you can fly. You will also start becoming more creative. If you have a lot of preconceived notions about the way things ought to be, you are not going to be open to the possibility that there may be some other way, some other path, or even some other outcome.

Paul has been headed in a certain direction because he wanted Outcome A, only to find part way down the path that Outcome B was a much better choice. Now if he remained committed to A, he would never get to B, so he had to be open to changing his mind. That is one of the hardest things for human beings do; changing your mind means, to some extent, you might have been wrong.

After being with a group of superintendents for six days in a row, Paul's fiancé said, "You know superintendents are really interesting creatures." Paul said, "Well, give me your spin on it." She said, "Well, they don't listen very much. They really hold fast to their opinions and try to force other people to go along with them." Paul laughed because there was so much truth to that. People who are in charge—not just superintendents but any CEO, anyone who is in a leadership position—get boxed in to the feeling that they are right most of the time. They start believing that their ideas are the ones that people should follow. Isn't that what leadership is all about—to lead other people? The pre-conceived mind-set for leaders is: "I come up with an idea, I get you to go along with it, and therefore I have led you." This may mean that leaders don't listen much to other people and don't remain open to others' ideas.

Robert Greenleaf offers another conception of leadership—the servant leader model, which says, "My job is to serve the people I work with, and by serving them I lead them." That is arguably the better model but not the more popular one, at least in today's climate.

Not holding fast to the need to be right, not holding fast to the idea that the outcome you seek must happen, allows for more creative expression and for growth to occur. When you know what the answer is supposed to be, neither you nor the people around you have much room to grow because there is no place to go.

In Paul's organization, a senior staff member didn't want to let go of power and authority because he was uncomfortable with relinquishing control. However, the need for everybody else to blossom required that he do just that. It was a major struggle between two different worldviews. Many leaders don't think that growth is important; to them, leadership is not about growth, it is about control. If you are about control, then the people around you will not grow. Enlightened leaders understand that growth is essential for improvement. Openness is a catalyst for promoting both growth and creativity. It is not the same as laissez-faire or anything goes—those are perversions of openness. Openness requires structure; it is not the absence of structure. It is a structured approach which, when done properly, produces great results by liberating people to be more creative and to find their higher potential.

What Might This Look Like in Practice?

Steve had a professor who taught him that leaders should build floors under people to support them, not ceilings over them: Ceilings limit the potential height people might reach. The same lesson can be gleaned from a flea circus. When flea trainers were training fleas to jump and they had them in a box, they would take the lid off, and the fleas could only jump as high as where the lid had been because the lack of openness had inhibited their ability to expand their skills beyond a certain level. In an organization that isn't open or doesn't have an open-minded leader, people's ability to grow and expand to their higher potential is limited. The message spreads through an organization quickly, and you get conformity rather than creativity from employees.

When Paul was superintendent in Princeton, there was an initiative to promote creativity. The school community was engaged in a process to figure out the kinds of kids they wanted to produce, namely: kids who were diverse thinkers, expansive in their thinking processes and creative, and divergent in their approach to learning and problem solving. District educators tried to figure out what they needed to do to produce that result. They decided to focus on classroom questions—how do teachers ask questions, and what level of questions were they using—because they decided that was the best way to foster creativity. Then, they realized that creativity is also about how the teachers handle student questions. Observers found that every time a student asked a divergent question in the classroom, it was quashed. The administrators said, "Well, this is terrific. We are encouraging divergence by squashing it at every opportunity." And of course, when you do that, you end up with compliance and conformity, not creativity.

Opportunities for growth continually occur in your personal and professional lives. Growth can be about little things as well as big things. Paul is trying to learn some new eating habits because people he respects tell him that it will be good for him. He is finding it hard to give up the Twinkies, but he's thinking about it and talking about it, and that is a good first step. For the first time since he was a child, Steve has started eating oatmeal. Steve's brother told him that oatmeal is good for you, and Steve figured out a way to make it taste good, not by putting sugar on it but by adding some fruit and almond slivers. Now, Steve has oatmeal at least once each week. Paul, on the other hand, is still rejecting it.

Steve is working with a trainer who encourages him and shows him how to do exercises he has never done before. For the first time in 15 years, he has taken up skiing again, and he is taking lessons so that he can have fun and minimize the risk of getting hurt. Steve's grown children are watching this. They're saying, "Wow! Dad is 60 years old, and he just took up skiing again, and last year he took up scuba diving." Steve didn't do this so he could serve as a role model for his sons, but, as a bonus, his sons got to see him as a lifelong learner.

In your personal or professional life or both, you have the opportunity to grow and learn from an almost limitless array of activities and endeavors that will enhance your life, if you are open. Or you can just go on doing what you did last year and the year before, a little like the movie *Groundhog Day*, in which you keep having the same experiences over and over ad nauseam. Life is more interesting when you seek out new experiences and activities. The key is to work on being more open, more of the time, about more things, expanding the circle of openness as much as possible. And if you do that, creativity and growth follow.

WHY OPENNESS IS THE KEY TO CREATING INFINITE POTENTIALITY

Openness is the key to everything. Enlightened leaders must have openness as their starting point because you can't turn on the lights unless you reach for the switch: Openness is the act of reaching. The possibility of infinite potentiality starts with that first step of reaching toward openness, a potentiality in so many different directions: growth, happiness, and fulfillment of possibilities. Openness also optimizes the potential to connect with a loved one or with family and to work with others as part of an organization. Certainly openness is the key to connecting with the Divine. Progress in all of these dimensions starts with willingness to be open. Willingness to be open means being willing to risk.

Paul travels to some fairly exotic places from time to time, and people always ask him, "Aren't you afraid?" The answer is no. He is respectful when he enters unfamiliar environments. He realizes he is not in Kansas anymore, that risks and potential dangers are involved. But being aware and taking precautions is different from being afraid. You lose your fear by beginning to trust the Universe, and you can show your trust in the Universe by being open to it. We firmly believe that the Universe is fundamentally good, but not every corner of it is. Clearly, there are dark spots, and you have to be aware of that. But being aware of it shouldn't shut you down. Having to deal with some bad people and bad experiences doesn't mean you have to be tainted by those experiences. If you are, you allow the bad people and bad experiences in your life to build fences around you, to create enclosures around your own happiness and your own potential. So you've got to knock those walls and those fences down—and you do that by being open.

While you must strive to keep your bad experiences from dampening your spirit, you can also use those experiences as opportunities for growth. Often you make progress in life, not in spite of the dangers around you but because of them. If you didn't have the challenges, if you didn't have difficult people, if you didn't have dangerous circumstances and trying times, you would not be able to focus on where you might go and what you might become. A sense of challenge creates possibility, and it creates the reward to a certain extent: The reward comes from doing something difficult, not something easy. Life, in part, is about overcoming the difficult, and to do that you have to be open.

Fear is the enemy of openness. It closes you down. Steve is proud of himself for trying to learn to ski again because since he had back surgery for a ruptured disk 15 years ago, the thought of going on a ski slope made him fearful. He decided he would try skiing again despite his fear. He would be prudent. He would go slow, take lessons, and exercise his body so that he would be more agile and fit. He would minimize the risk by preparing. Steve didn't lose his fear, he just decided that he would not let the fear stop him and that he would open himself to the experience. He wasn't doing so to show that he could act courageously, but in hindsight, it felt that way because courage is moving forward despite your fear. In the winter of 2004, Steve spent a week skiing in Steamboat Springs, Colorado, with his brother, his younger son, and his younger son's godparents. The skiing

Suggestions for Action

- Have discussions with your leadership team about the principle of openness.
- Ask the leadership team to identify areas where the organization would benefit by being more open.
- Invite the leadership team to share stories about the positive affects of creating more open climates and processes.
- Ask trusted members of your inner circle to help you identify areas where you would benefit from being more open.
- Declare your intention to increase openness in certain areas and invite feedback as to how well it is working.
- Look for an area where, through synchronicity or the principle of our unique life lessons, the Universe is letting you know you need to be open to making a significant change in your behavior or beliefs.

adventure created the circumstances for his younger son to relocate from Colorado to the east coast and to return to school after being away from home for 10 years. So, Steve's openness to return to skiing despite his fear created other openings for potentialities to manifest for his entire family.

Openness is the key, and a key is a powerful symbol. Keys unlock doors, and often we want the things behind those doors. Openness is a golden key, maybe even a magical key, which can unlock your potential. As a leader, you can give out these golden keys to yourself and to others so that everyone has access to unbounded potential. Openness is the golden key that opens all the doors. Enlightened leaders share their keys, give copies of their keys away. They don't hold them and say, "I'm the guy with the key and you can't have it." Instead, they make this golden key available so everyone can open doors and move forward.

SUMMARY

Openness is a fundamental principle of leadership and a fundamental principle of life itself. Your degree of openness at any given moment determines what you let in and what you let out. It determines what you let into your space and place, into your mind and heart, and into your very soul. It determines what you let out, where and under what circumstances, and to whom. You are in a continual dance with openness. Sometimes you lead; sometimes it leads. You can choose to move in the direction of openness. You can reflect and ask yourself if you are being open enough in any given situation or circumstance. You can use the world as a mirror to see how open you really are. As a leader, you can model openness and create open systems, and you can encourage and foster openness in others. As a leader, you can use openness to foster your own growth and the growth of others, as well as your own creativity and the creativity of others. Finally, you can use openness as a springboard to tap into and connect with the spiritual dimension of life.

The Principle of Trust

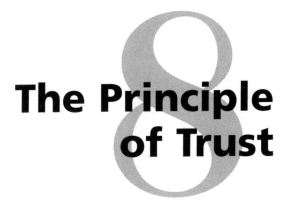

Trust is a fundamental principle of the spiritual dimension of leadership. It may well be the foundation on which everything else is built. Like motherhood and apple pie, it's a mainstay. Who doesn't want trust? In a group setting, ask people who don't want to be trusted to raise their hand. Look around the room. Not a single hand will go up. Everyone wants to be trusted and to be trustworthy, not only because it says something about who you are but also because it says something about the way others see you.

On a personal level, what can you trust yourself to do or not do, say or not say? On an interpersonal level, can you trust what people are saying to you? Can they trust what you are saying to them? Can they trust you to do X if they ask you to? Can you trust them to do X if they say they will? These are difficult questions, but it goes way beyond that:

Can you trust your spouse?

Can you trust your children?

Can you trust your friends?

Can you trust the organization you work for?

Can you trust our government?

Can you trust our nation?

Can you trust the Universe?

Can you trust the Divine? (Only people of faith have to address that one!)

Can you trust life itself?

Of course, while you may have a general predisposition in some of these areas, in reality such questions become even more complex when you consider: trust to do what and under what circumstances? Nonetheless, as a leader, you can't be effective without trust—which means learning to trust yourself and trust others. You can't be effective unless you are trustworthy and engender trust in your organization. Trust is to people as water is to plants—everyone needs just the right amount to thrive. As a leader, you are in a position to dispense a lot of trust—or not. One of the by-products of dispensing trust is that it is truly empowering, which is one of the reasons it is such a fundamental principle of enlightened leadership.

Of course, trust usually takes place in a context and is conditional. Leaders are continually making judgments about how much trust to give and under what circumstances. It is dispensed on a kind of cost/benefit, risk/reward basis. "I'll trust you with a hundred dollars." How about one thousand dollars? ten thousand dollars? one hundred thousand dollars? The circle of trust goes down as the cost goes up. With respect to a teenage son or daughter, when do you trust them to drive the family car? Does it make a difference if it is a clunker or brand new?

Trust is interesting. We have found that it is a little bit like love. When you give it, you receive it. The more you engender it, the more it grows and comes back to you. In the last chapter, we focused on the principle of openness. One of the principles you can be open to fostering in yourself and others is trust.

Steve remembers a time when, as superintendent, he felt a lack of trust between himself and the president of the teachers' union. A new union president was elected, and Steve saw it as an opportunity to build trust. He told the union president that he wanted to build the level of trust between them and asked her if she thought that was a worthy goal. Fortunately, the new president was open to Steve's invitation. Together, they established regular meetings and discussion sessions. They exchanged private phone numbers and agreed to call each other as soon as either of them heard something that might be problematic or sensitive to the other side. Steve shared some of his political concerns about information getting out to the membership prematurely or out of context. Deciding to begin the process of trust building by modeling, Steve demonstrated an increased level of trust by sharing some sensitive information with the union president, asking her to treat it confidentially and not to jump the gun on it. The union president responded in kind, not only by honoring Steve's trust but also by sharing sensitive information with Steve. Gradually the level of trust between them began to grow. As a by-product of the time they spent together, they started to appreciate one another as human beings and even started to like each other. As their relationship grew stronger and the trust level between them grew, it rippled out, and the entire organization benefited.

A few years later, sadly, the union president died suddenly. The year before she died, Steve had presented her with the superintendent's award for distinguished service. The union president's family said Steve would never know just how much that award meant to her. They told Steve they wanted to put it in her coffin, and they asked if he would have a replica made for the family to keep. Steve was touched by their request and arranged it. As he handed the plaque to a member of the family, Steve thought how far they had come in their circle of trust. Even in the telling of the story, the positive effects from that expanded circle of trust continue to flow.

WHY IT IS IMPORTANT FOR LEADERS TO BE TRUSTING

With respect to the spiritual dimension of leadership, there may not be anything more important than being trusting. It is hard to be positive or to have reverence if you are not trusting. Paramount to everything else, trust implies a sense of openness, of possibility, of acceptance, of detachment. The doorway of enlightened leadership opens through being trusting. Being trusting is the foundation of enlightened leadership on which the other floors are built. If you can't trust, it becomes difficult to practice and express the other spiritual principles of leadership. We are struck by how little trust there is among the leaders we meet. We are always hearing talk about how they have to do various things because they really can't trust people. There seems to be a perception that you have to guard against other people, you have to protect yourself, and you have to create boundaries and walls because, without those, you can't function. But every wall you build is a wall against trust. Every door you close and lock is a door against trust. Nonetheless, trust is where you have to start.

If you are among those who believe that everyone has a divine spark, then a place to start is to trust that it is there. Furthermore, embedded in that divine spark is an innate quality of goodness. You can trust that people are innately good and treat them accordingly, or you can use trust to nurture the inherent goodness and divine spark in people. The very act of trusting people unleashes a powerful force that empowers them and brings out the best in them. Trust, then, is the recognition of the Divine in someone else. Ultimately, that is what you are trusting: their higher self. You are not trusting their lower, ego-centered self because lower selves aren't very trustworthy—that's why they are lower.

When you interact with people, you choose what level you want to interact on, and they choose what level to respond on. The choice is to choose the higher self—which is divine and therefore much easier to trust—or the lower self, which is more base and therefore much harder to trust. Everyone has both sides; metaphorically, everyone lives in a two-story house. Do you want to go to the top floor or the bottom floor? That is the choice. When you are interacting with another person, you choose on which floor to be. Trust is about the choice you make, not about the other person. It is more about you being trusting than about the other person being trustworthy. When you initiate trusting energy and trusting behavior, it tends to bring out the trustworthy parts in the other person. If they want to interact with you, and you are going to live on the second floor, they've got to join you there. Most people are capable of climbing the stairs. We know that there are exceptions; we've dealt with a few people over the years who were incapable of leaving the bottom floor. But if you choose to go up to that higher floor, most folks will join you there most of the time. Some people may not respond as you hope or they may stay on the bottom floor (responding to their lower self), but it is important not to generalize from that— not to say, "Well, that proves what happens when you trust someone."

We subscribe to the values expressed in the following quote, which is widely attributed to Mother Teresa:

> People are often unreasonable, illogical, and self-centered; forgive them anyway. If you are kind, people may accuse you of selfish, ulterior motives; be kind anyway. If you are successful, you will win some false friends and some true enemies; succeed anyway. If you are honest and frank, people may cheat you; be honest and frank anyway. What you spend years building, someone may destroy overnight; build anyway. If you find serenity and happiness, they may be jealous; be happy anyway. The good you do today, people will often forget tomorrow; do good anyway. Give the world the best you have, and it may never be enough; give the world the best you've got anyway. You see, in the final analysis, it is all between you and God; it was never between you and them anyway.

The whole thrust of the quote is that you have a choice. Bad things may happen, but do the good thing anyway. People may disappoint you, but choose the higher road anyway. It is a powerful quote and exactly right because the choice is always yours. You have a choice to make about how you approach things. Do you choose to trust or not to trust? We have always tried to choose the trusting approach. What we have found is that nine times out of ten, people will respond in a trustworthy manner. One time out of ten, they will not, and in those cases, you may be hurt or damaged. Give us odds of nine to one anytime, and we are going to take them. How about you?

Not only are the odds in your favor, but also you acquire side benefits from giving your trust in terms of how people see themselves. Trust is a form of expectation; when people feel trusted, they tend to behave in a trustworthy manner and give more of themselves, not less. Being trusted helps their best selves to emerge. That goes back to the leadership question, because if you are in a leadership position, don't you want the most out of people? Don't you want to get their highest possible selves engaged in what's going on in the organization? Certainly an enlightened leader would. Then how do you do that? By distrusting them? By pointing out that they are not good people and not people who can be trusted, therefore, you will arrange to make them do things? Or is it by getting them to rise up to their higher potential? This may be the fundamental difference between good leaders and not-so-good leaders. Good leaders tend to trust, and the not-so-good leaders tend say people cannot be trusted, that they are fundamentally dishonest and bad, and therefore you have to guard against their behavior by making them do what's right—they won't make the right choices for themselves. The latter is a counterproductive approach to leadership, and from our perspective, it is not spiritually based. However, we see it happening in workplaces all the time. Those not-so-good leaders need to be encouraged to try a more trusting way. Trust isn't just a feeling, it is a choice.

When Steve shared some information with the president of the teacher's union that could have been used to harm Steve, he took a risk that she wouldn't betray a trust freely given. Trust doesn't always work, but the odds heavily favor the leader who chooses to initiate trust in others. One of the keys is letting people know that you are placing trust in them or trying to build trust with them, and then inviting them to live up to the trust that has been given.

What Might This Look Like in Practice?

Leaders who are not trusting do a lot of micromanaging and second-guessing because they think they cannot rely on anybody to do anything right. When you are in a situation where you view things that way, you've got a lot more work ahead of you. In an organization, the level of forward thrust is directly correlated with the level of trust the leader has in the organization. Trusting empowers. Distrust disempowers. When you empower people, things happen, and when you disempower them, things stop.

When Paul wanted to get something done in his organization, he would set the conditions by picking a team, giving them a charge, and then stepping out of the way, allowing the team members to do what he was trusting them to do. Early in his career, Paul worked for someone else as a principal. He was supposed to be

Suggestions for Action

- Expand your circle of trust to include someone you don't like and observe what happens.
- Use the principle of trust to build a more positive relationship with someone.
- Create an ad hoc team; give them an important task with a written charge; tell them you trust them to do a first-rate job on it and then get out of the way.
- Give trust as a gift to a person or group with Goal A in mind. Notice how they not only give you Goal A but surprise you by doing more than you expected, and come back having achieved Goals B and C as well.

setting up a certain kind of activity with his staff, and that afternoon, he showed up at the superintendent's office. The superintendent asked what he doing there. Paul answered, "I wanted to check some personnel files of a few of my staff members." The superintendent asked if this wasn't the day the team was supposed to start working. Paul said, "Yeah, they are." The superintendent wondered why he wasn't back at the school to guide them. Paul responded: "I picked the team, and I gave them the task. I picked the job. It will come out where it is supposed to come out." And the superintendent just looked at Paul as though he had lost his mind. Of course, Paul was absolutely right. It came out exactly where it was supposed to come out. Most of the time, that is going to happen.

In baseball, if you get a hit in three out of ten turns at bat, you are a candidate for the Hall of Fame. In organizations, when you trust, our experience is that you will bat six or seven out of ten, a much higher percentage than a Hall of Fame slugger. Why would you not do that?

WHY IT IS ESSENTIAL FOR LEADERS TO BE TRUSTWORTHY

It is essential for leaders to be trustworthy, among other things, because they are role models. Acting in a trustworthy manner encourages others to behave in the same way. If you are not trustworthy yourself, it doesn't provide the impetus for other people to behave in that manner. In organizations and human interactions, there is an interplay between the way one starts and the way the other responds. If an exchange starts in a negative way, then the response tends to be negative, too. If an exchange starts in a positive way, the response tends to be positive. So if you are looking for trustworthiness in others, you start by being trustworthy yourself. Whatever you sow, you'll reap. If you want trust, you've got to be trustworthy.

Integrity and trustworthiness are inextricably tied to one another—you can't have one without the other. If you are trustworthy, you live your integrity. People can rely on your word, on your commitments, and on your goodwill in seeking to act in ways that will benefit them, or at the very least, not be harmful to them. Let's take a closer look at the word *integrity*. It is a close cousin of the word *integrated*. Integrity at its core connotes a sense of being integrated. When you are integrated, all of the pieces fit. When you are dealing with someone who you don't trust, something doesn't fit right. There is something out of sync. Even though most of what they say or do makes sense, something doesn't quite match. Everyone knows people whose words and affect do not match up. Somehow you know that these people are putting on a false face and can't be trusted.

Paul started teaching in North Carolina in the 1960s, right after schools were racially integrated. Suddenly, a lot of teachers were teaching kids of another race. Paul remembers a white teacher struggling one day in a class that had a lot of African-American kids. She was telling the kids, "I don't know why you don't feel better about this class, why you don't feel good about me—you know I really love you." One of the little African-American kids said, "Well, if you love me, why don't you tell your face." He knew that something didn't quite match up between this teacher's face and her words.

Without a sense of trustworthiness, of integration, there's always something that doesn't ring true. Like the little African-American child, enlightened leaders are attuned to what does and doesn't ring true; ringing is all about attunement—it is either on key or off key. When something is off key, it is out of sync or dissonant, and you pick that up if you are attuned to it.

What Might This Look Like in Practice?

Where leaders lack trust in themselves, and therefore are not worthy of being trusted by other people, they revert to a form of leadership that is heavy-handed and coercive. They also tend to see the world as a zero sum game: Somehow if I can diminish you, I can be enhanced; I'll knock you down, so I'll be higher than you. This is in contrast to a worldview that says, if you are enhanced, I'm enhanced—the win-win view.

Paul had a staff member whose worldview lacked trust. He even explained to Paul one day, "You don't get it. If they win, you lose." Or, "If you win, they lose. There can only be one winner and one loser." At the time, Paul was experiencing a lot of conflict with the board. Some of its members were, arguably, out to get Paul. This staff member called a special meeting after work with a consultant to plot how they could get the people who were out to get Paul. He said to Paul, "Listen, it's either you or them. If you don't take them down, they're going to take you down. And you've got to decide." To which Paul replied, "You know what? No, I don't. I don't have to decide that. I'm going

> ### Suggestions for Action
>
> - Use self-disclosure to reveal some of your shortcomings, showing your softer, human side as a work in progress.
> - Remember that being trustworthy gives people a reason to follow you.
> - In an area where you are trying to grow as a leader, declare your intention and invite feedback from others regarding your progress.
> - Tell your staff that you believe trust is an important principle of leadership and that you want to foster trust throughout the organization.
> - Remember that trustworthiness grows out of the alignment between the things you espouse and the things you actually do, so strive to align your walk and your talk.
> - Remember that when your walk and talk are aligned, your personal power increases.

to be who I am, and I'm going to be what I am, and take whatever the consequences are. But I'm not going to become somebody else and do something just like the people who I don't think are doing the right thing. If I have to become like them to survive, I would rather not survive. Thank you very much, this meeting is over." Paul not only trusted himself, he trusted the Universe as well, and in time, it became very clear that his trust was well placed.

WHY IT IS IMPORTANT TO TRUST YOURSELF

How are you going to trust anyone else if you don't trust yourself? You can't do anything for someone else that you can't do for yourself first. There is absolutely no way to create a trusting environment for other people if you don't have some trust in yourself. Now the follow-up questions are: How do you learn to trust yourself? And where do you look to learn that? A place to start is to ask yourself why, in terms of your life experiences, you don't trust yourself. Then look at what you can do to modify those things that are causing you not to trust yourself. Perhaps you don't trust yourself because you haven't been trustworthy. Sometimes it is hard to see yourself, so counseling may be needed to learn where some of those feelings come from. We don't think you can begin to trust yourself without some insight as to why you *don't* trust yourself. People who have tried a lot of things and failed may not trust themselves because when they did, things didn't work out. From a spiritual perspective, perhaps such people haven't been looking in the right places within themselves. They may have to search within through meditation or some other introspective process to try to get in touch with who they are. Maybe what they are not trusting is that they are operating in a way that is inconsistent with who they really are, but they don't know it.

You are what you are. Therefore, you have to accept what you are at any point in time—and part of what you are is a work in progress. Nobody's perfect. None of the people watching you is perfect either. The world is made up of a lot of imperfect people trying to move forward. A lot of trusting yourself is just understanding that people are all engaged in this process. No one is going to get it all right all the time. There is no point in worrying about the fact that you are going to make mistakes. A mistake is a potential lesson anyway. So what if you do make a mistake? Learn from it and grow from it. It is usually not the end of the world. Even if it is the end of the world, you are not going to be around to notice afterward anyway.

Let's return to where we started. You cannot love someone else unless you first love yourself, and that principle applies to many aspects of life, including trust. Your ability to give anything, whether it is love or trust or something else, starts with your having it to give. You can start by first giving it to yourself. Trust is a choice as well as a feeling. You can choose to trust yourself. When you give trust to yourself so that you will be able to give it to others, you are not being selfish.

There is a fairly narrow line between being selfish or self-centered and being accepting and trusting and loving toward yourself. The balance tips toward self-centeredness when you are too focused on yourself—people who love themselves to excess are considered narcissistic. Paul has found a good balance by being self-critical. He is very hard on himself, often knowing when he has fallen short and acknowledging that to himself. On the other hand, his saving grace is that he also accepts himself. He has an inner dialogue which says, "You really screwed that one up, dude." And then he says, "Well, maybe next time you'll do better, and it is OK because you're still learning." And so he points out the flaw and accepts the humanity of being a flawed person, and then he moves on. You need to have this type of inner dialogue to create the proper balance between being self-centered and self-aware. If you're too self-centered, you probably aren't having much of a dialogue with yourself. There is a constant dance between being inside yourself and outside yourself, and if you're going to be balanced, you need to be stepping back and forth all the time. If you're not stepping back and forth, then in all likelihood you'll find yourself out

> ### Suggestions for Action
>
> - Don't be afraid to ask foolish questions because foolish questions can open up real dialogue. You can even say, "This may sound foolish, but . . ."
> - Trust is truly a choice, so choose to trust yourself.
> - Declare your intention to trust yourself, or at least to trust yourself more.
> - Practice trusting yourself in a particular area of your life. Ask trusted friends or trusted colleagues to give you feedback and serve as your mirror.
> - Take the road to self-trust. The more you take it, the more familiar it will be.

of balance. If you are standing inside of the circle all the time or on the outside all of the time, you are out of balance; hopping back and forth between the inside and outside of the circle allows you to create a balance between being self-approving and self-aware and being so self-centered that you are narcissistic and selfish. One aspect of being an enlightened leader is being able to move in and out of the circle and not being stuck in either place.

What Might This Look Like in Practice?

For as long as Paul can remember, people have accused him of being over-confident. He has tried to analyze that feedback; sometimes he is accused of being arrogant because of that confidence. Hearing this from others always struck him as curious because he never felt arrogant internally. He decided that this perception that he is overconfident or arrogant has to do with his willingness to judge himself and not to be judged by others or to accept others' judgment about him. When he gives a speech or participates in a meeting or does something on television, he analyzes for himself how he did. Sometimes he feels he did well and is happy about it, and sometimes he feels that he could have done better one way or another, and he thinks about how he needs to do it differently next time. Of course, he also gets feedback from others, but if the feedback doesn't align with his own judgment, either good or bad, he tends not to worry about it.

The bottom line is that Paul focuses on self-approval rather than the approval of others. Many people have been raised with a lot of parental judgment and judgment by other adults, and they grow up never getting past that to the point where they sit in judgment of themselves rather than allowing others to judge them. When you can judge yourself, you are starting to trust yourself, and you gain a tremendous amount of personal power. As long as you give your power over to somebody else by allowing that person to sit in judgment of you, you cannot be true to your self and act in an independent way.

TRUSTING YOUR HIGHER SELF

We encourage you to recognize, or at least be open to, the idea that you have a higher self. Your higher self, sometimes called your soul or divine spark, is available to you for guidance. It is an infinite fountain of wisdom that comes from a divine source, which is readily available if you choose to access it. When you do, you receive guidance from the Universe, either internally or externally, or both. Your higher self is the divine aspect of yourself. It is your connection to the Divine, which means that everyone has access to divine wisdom. And if you can't trust divine wisdom, what can you trust?

There are many ways of seeking divine guidance. One is through your higher self by simply asking for it. Just as there are many ways of seeking divine guidance, the guidance you receive may take many forms. At times, you can get a strong feeling that something is right or not right for you. Sometimes you receive flashes of intuition, or messages in a dream state, or in a meditative state, or when practicing a religious ritual. At times, you receive guidance through other people or synchronistic events. It is not always easy to know when you are receiving the guidance you seek. It may come at surprising times and in surprising ways: in a book or article that you are reading or in a movie you are watching; from a friend or a stranger. Once you ask for guidance, you need to be alert to what comes to you, and you need to trust that you will receive it. The hard part is recognizing the guidance because sometimes it is subtle and sometimes you may think you are getting conflicting guidance from different sources. We are not advocates of blind trust. To the extent that it is possible, you need to verify and reality-test what you believe is the divine guidance you are receiving. Take it for a test drive, check it out, see if it feels right, and see if it is working. If it is not working, you may be misreading the advice or misapplying it or assuming that something is coming from a divine source when it is not.

What Might This Look Like in Practice?

When Steve sits down to write, he first seeks guidance from his higher self. What he says is prayerlike in tone. For example, as he is about to write an article on a topic like "Nourishing Our Spirit as Leaders," he may say something like, "I ask my higher self to guide and inform me. I seek inspiration and insight. May my words be interesting, engaging, informative, inspiring, and useful to those who read them. May my words carry the energy of divine light, love, wisdom, and truth."

Paul is less direct in his approach. Paul centers himself and quiets his mind. He then allows images, stories, and metaphors to cross the barrier from his unconscious mind into his conscious mind. (Your higher self resides in the unconscious recesses of your psyche.) Paul then relies on his intuitive mind to guide him in the words he writes and the stories he tells. Both Steve and Paul believe they receive guidance from their respective higher selves, but their approaches for doing so are very different.

You can enlist guidance not only from your own higher self but also from the higher selves of others. An analogy of the way this process works would be like a listserv on the World Wide Web. As a member of a listserv, you can pose a question to all of the members of the listserv and receive guidance from those who choose to respond. Your higher self can enlist the cooperation and support of the higher selves of others to bring you certain information and insights. This is one reason that the guidance people seek often comes from others. Again, the hard part is to recognize that you are receiving an answer to a question that you have generated, either consciously or unconsciously.

How else do you get to your higher self, and how do you know when you are operating in relation to your lower self, which is ego centered? When you have an emotional response to something, that emotional response may or may not be coming from your higher self. Clearly, it is an indication that you have a strong feeling about something. However, if you then can create a little bit of space by practicing detachment until the emotion passes, then you can apply your higher thinking processes and will more likely make a better decision. Sometimes something makes you angry. Perhaps someone has done something inappropriate, and you need to respond in a way that tells them so. Distancing and practicing detachment allows you to respond from a higher place. People are always telling kids to count to ten when they feel angry, but leaders have to do more than that. You can "sleep on it," postponing action until you are rested and in a more relaxed state. You can pray on it or meditate on it until you become more centered, and then you are more likely to be able to come at it from a higher place.

Steve received an e-mail that pushed his buttons and made him angry. He wrote down some of his initial reactions, but he just did it in rough draft form, enough to capture all of the major points and his responses to them. He didn't formalize it, and he didn't send it. When he looked at it a couple of days later, he decided that what he had written had merit and validity but, in looking at the situation from a larger context, he thought it was better not to send the response. Sometimes coming from your higher self means seeing things from a larger context, whereas reacting viscerally means seeing things from a narrower focus. In other words, even when your reactions are based on truth, when you can step back to a rested, more centered place, you can see it in a larger context. You might say, "You know, given all of the things going on in this person's life, I don't think this is something that needs to be addressed right now. This isn't the way they normally function, so because of the circumstances, I'm going to let this one go, or at least for now."

Part of going to your higher self is being able to step back and look at the world in a bigger context, but it is also being able to look at yourself from the outside as though you are an observer. Again, you can do that only by disconnecting from the emotional reaction that most people have to things. If you can step back after sleeping on it and then try to observe what is going on from the outside, you'll likely select a different course of action than when you are trapped inside a whirlwind of emotion. Leaders are often attacked, or they are playing referee between people attacking each other. Being able to get a handle on it all becomes important. It is the old notion of "get a grip." Sometimes you just don't have a grip on things, and they slip through your fingers because you have allowed your emotions to take over when you should be more dispassionate about what is going on. The more relaxed and centered you are, the more access you will have to your higher self and your own inner wisdom.

Often when you check with your higher self, it is not about what you do regarding somebody else. Rather, it is about what you do regarding yourself because you are the only person you ever *have* to live with. You don't have

Suggestions for Action

- Remember that the road suggested by your higher self is the better one, but often, it is "the road less traveled" because it is the more difficult one.
- When you are resolving a problem, ask yourself whether you are taking the low road or the high road.
- When you are not in a good frame of mind, don't write the memo you feel like writing or make the phone call you feel like making until you have reflected on it.
- Ask your higher self for guidance and then remain open for the guidance to manifest.

to live with anybody else, but you do have to live with yourself. Remember the adage: "No matter where you go, there you are." The one person you can't get away from is yourself. Therefore, when you make choices about how you are going to act, you need to be comfortable with those choices. If your choice is against your higher self, you are deciding to live in foreign territory, and you end up being less happy as a result. When leaders make the wrong choice about which road to take, they affect not only themselves but their organization and the people in it. Conversely, when you make a choice that is aligned with your higher self, you feel happier and more satisfied, as well. The road you selected positively affects your organization and empowers and uplifts the people in it.

ENLIGHTENED LEADERS MUST LEARN TO TRUST THE UNIVERSE

In the context of this work, we use the words *Universe* and *Divine* interchangeably. Figuratively, the higher self whispers in your right ear, and the Universe whispers in your left ear. They both send you signals that you may not listen to most of the time, or at least not as much as you should or could.

You should learn to trust the Universe because the Universe is always right by definition. It is bigger than you are. It is more powerful than you are. It has been around longer, and it knows a lot more. When you come to a point when you can trust that, then you align yourself with a power much greater than yourself. That is the higher view. The lower view and more practical view is you can't stand against the Universe. You are never going to be able to beat the Universe at its game. You are too small for that. So you have only one choice in our book, and that is to trust it; to not trust it is to fight against it, and that is a losing proposition.

This worldview hit home with Paul when he was on a trip to Peru. On a boat on the Amazon River, he saw the banks caving, and he asked one of the Peruvians, "What do you guys do about dealing with the river when it does this thing?" The man looked at Paul and said, "Sir, the river goes where it will." Paul was going to play engineer and dam it up or something, ignoring the fact that the river was a force of nature that was not to be controlled by him or anybody else. The Universe is the ultimate force of nature, and the Universe goes where it will. You can either go with the flow, or you can fight it, but it is a fight you are always going to lose. If you happen to believe, as we do, that the Universe is also infinitely intelligent, then why not start to trust where it is taking you?

We trust the Universe. We know people who don't trust it at all and even think there is nothing there to trust. Of course, others would place themselves somewhere along that continuum. We suggest you look back at the way events have played out in different aspects of your life. By looking backward, you may be able to see some of the patterns that have created opportunities for your growth, the lessons you have learned, and opportunities to use your innate gifts. Look backward and see what has happened: things you didn't think were going to be good for you turned out to be very good. At the time, you didn't think it was good—the job you didn't get, the house you wanted to buy but lost to someone else, the relationship you lost. At the time, you wouldn't have made those choices for yourself, and yet, looking backward, you can see that these events were positive factors in your life. We are not saying that many of these crossroads weren't difficult or stressful or painful—only that, ultimately, they were good for you, helping you become the person you are today. Realizing that these patterns and processes are still unfolding in your life may help you join the ranks of those of us who trust the Universe.

What Might This Look Like in Practice?

Younger people look at Paul's career, and they say, "Wow, it's so well thought out. It's so perfectly sequenced. How did you do that? When you were young, how did you know to do that?" Paul just laughs because he never planned any of it—and he couldn't have. If someone had told him when he went to his first American Association of School Administrators conference in 1971 that in a little more than 20 years he'd be running that organization, he would have found that laughable; at the time, he hadn't even been a principal. There was no way to plan how to end up in that place, but the Universe took him there. All he did was go with the flow by accepting things as they happened and recognizing that one thing leads to another. In the Robert Frost poem entitled "Nothing Gold Can Stay," there is a line that says, "So dawn goes down to day." Each dawn changes into day; things are always changing, one event always leading to another. That is just the way life is. You have to accept that the flow will work to your benefit in the long run, even though at times you are going to be highly dubious about that from your present vantage point. If you'd asked Paul at the time if going through a breakup with his fiancé was a good thing, because he trusts the Universe he would have thought philosophically, "Well, it must be the right thing, I just don't know why." At the time, he accepted what was happening. He didn't understand it, and he didn't like it much—how could it be right when it hurt so much? Retrospectively, however, he can see that the breakup was only temporary, and ultimately it allowed the relationship to move forward to a much higher plane. In hindsight, he knows his trust in the Universe was well founded.

We count ourselves among those who believe that the Universe—the Divine—is perfect. It is not the Universe that is broken; rather, it is the world. This brings us back to the issue of trust again. Do you trust that belief? If you do, you will behave differently than if you don't think the Universe is perfect or at least well intentioned. You choose your worldview. If you think the Universe is essentially dark, hostile, or indifferent, your behavior will be markedly different. Enlightened leadership differs fundamentally from unenlightened leadership in this area. Unenlightened leadership has a dark universal view of things. The light has gone out. Such leaders view things as hostile and negative. Paul has worked with such people. They have a cynical view; when issues come up, these people go to that view and say things like: "Someone's out to screw us." "There's a trick here." "This isn't going to work." "We've got to be careful." "We've got to protect ourselves." And then Paul tries to present the opposing view: "Well, it could be OK. Why don't we think the best of these folks? Why do we assume that they're out to get us? Now we know that in some cases, people are out to screw us. But again, how much of the time? And sometimes, even if they're out to screw us, if we behave in a different way, if we behave as if they're not, sometimes they shift their behavior."

In any interaction, each party is looking toward the other; when they see you act in a positive way, often they will respond in kind. You have to be willing to put the first block down so that the next block can be put on top of it. If you are not willing to put the first block down, there is no way to get the second block down. The choice you can make is always to put the first block down. Somebody has to do it; it has to start someplace. If you are waiting for someone else to do it, it may never happen. But what you do know is if you put it down first, the first block is going to go down. That block becomes the foundation. Yes, maybe someone won't put another block on top of it, and maybe it will be the only block lying there, but at least you've done your part. But if you haven't put the first block down, suddenly you have moved the power from you to someone else.

> ## Suggestions for Action
>
> - Make a conscious choice to increase your trust in the Universe.
> - Demonstrate your choice through your thoughts, words, and deeds.
> - Ask the Universe to assist you in specific ways that contribute to serving others.
> - Ask the Universe to guide you.
> - Ask the Universe to increase your wisdom and effectiveness as a leader.
> - Ask the Universe to support you in the important work that you do.
> - Ask the Universe to help you manifest the fullest expression of your being.

If you choose to trust, to have an enlightened view, then you are always willing to make the first move. People who want to have real power in the world always move first rather than waiting for the other person to move so they can respond. The first move of an enlightened leader is to act in a positive, trusting way.

When you do that, you are in effect demonstrating trust in your fellow human beings, which is a form of trusting the Universe. We hope your experience will be sufficiently positive that you'll do it again. And even if it's negative, you'll try it again and learn that in the long run, Mother Teresa was wise: "If they are no longer trustworthy, trust anyway. People will disappoint you, but trust them anyway."

WHY IT IS IMPORTANT TO GIVE
TRUST AS A GIFT WHENEVER POSSIBLE

Trust is that first block you put down. That is the gift you give, the starting point. Paul loves to give gifts, and he used to love to *get* gifts. He's at the point now that he receives them graciously but he doesn't expect them, and therefore, he's always pleasantly surprised when they come. When he expected them, he never got anything more than he expected, and if he didn't get them, he was disappointed. Somewhere along the line, and he doesn't know why, he stopped expecting gifts from people. And interestingly, around the time he stopped expecting gifts, he started being much more giving. To Paul, one of the greatest gifts of all is the ability to give gifts. He loves to surprise people and give them things that they don't know are coming.

He remembers a weekend when he took a woman friend four or five different little presents. None of them were a big deal, but during the course of the two days he spent with her, he would say, "Oh, by the way I've got a surprise for you"—and he'd pull out one of the gifts. To see her face and the pleasure and gratitude for whatever that he had picked to give her was wonderful. Paul feels he got more out of it than she did. She was getting the present, but he got the real gift. Paul remembers learning in childhood that it is more blessed to give than to receive. His own life experience has confirmed that it's true.

Steve is fortunate that his mother and in-laws truly modeled the joy of giving and created wonderful role models for him in terms of demonstrating extraordinary generosity. You have to be careful when you are near his mother because, if you admire anything in her domain, her first inclination is to hand it to you with joy. The fact that she has something that somebody else might like to have is all the impetus she needs to give it away. Once you experience those types of role models, you want to do the same for others.

One of the most precious gifts people can give others is their trust. When you are a leader in an organization, some people say, "I'll give you trust when you earn it." The reality is that there simply isn't enough time for everybody to earn your trust. But you can give it anyway, as a gift. What greater gift is there than the gift of trust? It is almost priceless.

Suppose someone comes to you seeking permission to do something, and you say, "I don't need all the details. I trust you. Just do it. Just take care of it." They look at you with a questioning expression that says, "You do?" They want to see if you really mean it. And you say, "Yes, I do. I trust you." In that exquisite moment, they have a palpable reaction that at times seems almost transformative.

Trust is a fundamental principle not only of leadership but of life itself. Many life lessons revolve around the issue of trust. A woman Paul was dating had lost a couple of husbands through death and parting. How do you hold on to trust when you've experienced abandonment? Paul recognized intuitively, with the help of his higher self, that although she was a superficially open person and very warm, she had walls around her, and he told her so. "Most people don't know I have those," she said. Paul answered, "But that's OK because I'm going to just plow right through them." After the first or second week they were seeing each other, she looked at Paul and said, "You are knocking all my walls down, aren't you?" A little later, she became defensive about some issue, and Paul said, "Those are walls. Go ahead because you realize that I'm standing on the inside watching you build it." She started laughing. "Yes you are, aren't you?" she said. "I guess I shouldn't bother, huh." Paul said, "Well, help yourself, you aren't going to keep me out because this is all around the issue of trust." He went on to say, "The interesting thing is that by knocking down your walls, the contract I've made you is that it's going to be safe, because if it's not going to be safe for you, I have no right to knock your wall down." To the extent that Paul failed to make her safe, the whole chain of trust would be broken. In this story, Paul was declaring that he was trustworthy. He was seeking his friend's trust as a gift both to him and to her. He was asking her to make herself vulnerable and take a risk that he would not hurt her if she let her wall down. She took the risk and gave her trust as a gift. Over time, it became apparent that her trust was well placed.

What does it mean when we say, "Give trust as a gift?" What are the implications of that gift? for you? for the other person? Obviously, things may go well or not. You may trust someone to handle things in your absence, and that person may not do the job as well as you were hoping. How you respond to that outcome demonstrates what you meant when you said, "I'll trust you." As a leader, do you mean it or not? Do you just say it and, if the person falls short, jump all over them? Did you really mean it then? Or do you come back and say, "I trust you; I understand that sometimes things don't work out quite the way we had planned or hoped, so let's figure out what we can learn from this, but I want you to know that I still have faith in you, and I still trust you." You must remember that trust is not a simple act, complete once it is bestowed. It is an iterative and interactive process that builds through continual reflection and growth. It is an ongoing process where you continually demonstrate that your trust is true.

What Might This Look Like in Practice?

Trust is empowering, but it is also a heavy gift to give someone. Some people don't want it. Some people say, "Thanks, but no thanks; don't trust me with that responsibility." When Paul had been superintendent in Princeton for a year, one of the principals came into his office and said, "You know I've never worked as hard in my life as I've worked this year, and I just came in to ask you how you did it." Paul said, "What do you mean, 'how I did it?'" The principal said, "I have felt such pressure this year to perform, and I look back on the year and you never told me that I had to, you never forced me, but I felt such pressure from you to do the right thing, and I realized it's because you trusted me to do it." He went on to say, "I have never experienced such pressure in my life as what I had this year, to know that you were trusting me to do what I needed to do." And Paul laughed to himself. At the time, Paul was 32 years old and didn't have a clue about the deeper meaning of what he was doing. But the fact was that the principal was right. Paul let the principal know that he believed in him, laying out his expectations and trusting that the principal would do what he was capable of doing. Believing in someone else—expressing trust—can put a heavy load on him or her, particularly if it's a new experience. If people are used to being in a distrustful environment, it is much easier for them to operate in that environment, even though it's destructive and unhealthy; they know where the boundaries are. Conversely, in a trusting environment, the boundaries are limitless.

Enlightened leaders must not only model trust but also help some people learn how to accept it, help them carry that load. On many occasions in his career, people have said to Paul, "Just tell me what to do." He asks them, "Why?" They typically respond: "Because you're the boss." And he tells them, "Well, aren't you capable of deciding what you need to do without me telling you?" The dialogue goes back and forth:

"Well, I don't know."

"I think you do, that's why you're in that job you're in, so go do what you need to do."

"You're not going to tell me what to do?"

"No, I'm not going to tell you."

That's really hard for some people, but others will just soar in response. For the latter group, a little bit of trust can go a long way because they've just been waiting for someone to take the chains off. For others, you are teaching them to trust themselves.

Teaching people to trust themselves is not easy, especially if they've been conditioned not to do so. It is like the story where the zookeeper puts a chain on the elephant's leg to keep it from getting loose. The elephant tries to get loose and as it pulls against the chain, it hurts its leg. The elephant tries a number of times, and each time it scrapes its leg. After a time, the zookeeper puts a lighter chain on, and then a lighter one. As times goes by, the chain is replaced with a rope and finally with a piece of twine. Even though the elephant could break the twine easily, it's been trained not to do it. The elephant accepts the limitations that have been imposed and stops trying to break loose. That's what happens to people when they've been in an environment of distrust for a long period of time: They stop trying to break out, to break the chain. If an enlightened leader comes along and says, "Hey, run around," they say, "I can't run around. What do you mean making me run? It's going to hurt if I try to run around. If I try to get loose, I'm going to scrape my leg."

Creating a culture of trust can be difficult. One of the things enlightened leaders have to do is look at their organization and determine where it is in terms of its history, and where people are in terms of their history, and how capable they are of taking the trust that you want to give them. To some extent, you have to train people to accept your gift of trust. Until you do that, you won't be able to take your organization where you want to take it—into its brightest future.

SUMMARY

Trust is an empowering bond that empowers you and those you lead. Enlightened leaders continually strive to expand their circle of trust. They start by trusting themselves and then operate from a base of integrity, which makes them trustworthy. Enlightened leaders understand that trust is not just a feeling but also a choice. You can choose to trust and be trusting, but trust should not be given blindly. Trust must always be reality tested and tempered accordingly. One of the ways leaders expand their circle of trust is by trusting others and giving their trust to others as a gift as often as possible. Trusting others enhances their self-concept and facilitates their growth as part of their organization and as people. People who are trusted become more trusting, and they, in turn, further expand the circle of trust. Ultimately, enlightened leaders learn to trust not only their higher selves—the spark of divinity within—but also the Universe itself.

Selected Bibliography

Albom, M. (1997). *Tuesdays with Morrie.* New York: Doubleday.

Bronowski, J. (1973). *The ascent of man.* Boston: Little, Brown.

Bruyere, R. L. (1989). *Wheels of light.* New York: Fireside.

Campbell, J., with B. Moyers. (1988). *The power of myth.* New York: Doubleday.

Chambers, S. (2000). *Kabalistic healing.* Los Angeles: Keats.

Chopra, D. (1994). *Ageless body, timeless mind.* New York: Crown.

Chopra, D. (1994). *The seven spiritual laws of success.* San Rafael, CA: Amber-Allen.

Collins, J. (2001). *Good to great.* New York: Harper Collins.

Covey, S. R. (1990). *Principle-centered leadership.* New York: Summit Books.

Crichton, M. (1988). *Travels.* New York: Ballantine.

Crum, T. F. (1987). *The magic of conflict.* New York: Simon & Shuster.

Deal, T. E. (1995). *Leading with soul.* San Francisco: Jossey-Bass.

Dyer, W. W. (1992). *Real magic.* New York: Harper.

Dyer, W. W. (1998). *Wisdom of the ages.* New York: Avon Books.

Dyer, W. W. (2001). *There's a spiritual solution to every problem.* New York: Harper Collins.

Dyer, W. W. (2004). *The power of intention.* Carlsbad, CA: Hay House.

Farson, R. (1996). *Management of the absurd.* New York: Simon & Shuster.

Ferguson, M. (1980). *The Aquarian conspiracy.* Boston: Houghton Mifflin.

Fullan, M. (2001). *Leading in a culture of change.* San Francisco, CA: Jossey-Bass.

Fullan, M. (2003). *The moral imperative of school leadership.* Thousand Oaks, CA: Corwin.

Gawain, S. (1978). *Creative visualization.* New York: MJF Books.

Gladwell, M. (2005). *Blink.* New York: Little, Brown.

Gleick, J. (1987). *Chaos.* New York: Penguin.

Green, B. (1999). *The elegant universe.* New York: W. W. Norton.

Hawking, S. (2001). *The universe in a nutshell.* New York: Bantam Books.

Hawkins, D. R. (2002). *Power vs. force.* Carlsbad, CA: Hay House.

Heider, J. (1986). *The Tao of leadership.* New York: Bantam Books.

Hoyle, J. (2001). *Leadership and the force of love.* Thousand Oaks, CA: Sage.

Jackson, P. (1995). *Sacred hoops.* New York: Hyperiod.

Jaworski, J. (1996). *Synchronicity: The inner path of leadership.* San Francisco: Berrett-Koehler.

Kessler, R. (2000). *The soul of education.* Alexandria, VA: Association for Supervision and Curriculum Development.

Lenz, F. (1995). *Surfing the Himalayas.* New York: St. Martin's.

Markova, D. (2005). *The smart parenting revolution.* New York: Random House.

Millman, D. (1980). *Way of the peaceful warrior.* Tiburon, CA: H. J. Kramer.

Millman, D. (1993). *The life you were born to live.* Tiburon, CA: H. J. Kramer.

Myss, C. (1996). *Anatomy of the spirit.* New York: Harmony.

Myss, C. (2003). *Sacred contracts.* New York: Random House.

Nouwen, H. J. M. (1992). *The return of the prodigal son.* New York: Doubleday.

Peck, M. S. (1978). *The road less traveled.* New York: Simon & Shuster.

Peters, T., & Waterman, R. (1982). *In search of excellence.* New York: Harper & Row.

Ponce, C. (1991). *Kabbalah.* Illinois: Theosophical Publishing House.

Quinn, D. (1995). *Ishmael.* New York: Bantam.

Redfield, J. (1993). *The celestine prophecy.* New York: Warner.

Redfield, J. (1996). *The tenth insight.* New York: Warner.

Redfield, J. (1999). *The secret of Shambhala.* New York: Warner.

Remen, R. N. (2000). *My grandfather's blessings.* New York: Riverhead Books.

Ruiz, D. M. (1997). *The four agreements.* San Rafael, CA: Amber-Allen.

Schiller, M., Holland, B. M., & Riley, D. (Eds.). (2001). *Appreciative leaders: In the eye of the beholder.* Chagrin Falls, OH: The Taos Institute.

Senge, P., Scharmer, C. O., Jaworski, J., & Flowers, B. S. (2004). *Presence.* Cambridge, MA: Society for Organizational Learning.

Sharamon, S., & Baginski, B. J. (1991). *The chakra-handbook.* Wilmot, WI: Lotus Light.

Simpson, L. (1999). *The book of chakra healing.* New York: Sterling.

Thompson, S. (2005). *Leading from the eye of the storm.* Lanham, MD: Rowman & Littlefield Education.

Waitley, D. (1983). *Seeds of greatness.* New York: Simon & Shuster.

Wheatley, M. J. (1992). *Leadership and the new science.* San Francisco: Berrett-Koehler.

Wilkinson, B. (2000). *The prayer of Jabez.* Sisters, OR: Multnomah.

Zukav, G. (1989). *The seat of the soul.* New York: Fireside.

Zukav, G. (2000). *Soul stories.* New York: Simon & Shuster.

CORWIN PRESS

The Corwin Press logo—a raven striding across an open book—represents the union of courage and learning. Corwin Press is committed to improving education for all learners by publishing books and other professional development resources for those serving the field of PreK–12 education. By providing practical, hands-on materials, Corwin Press continues to carry out the promise of its motto: **"Helping Educators Do Their Work Better."**